Desert and Shepherd in Our Biblical Heritage

Nogah Hareuveni

Translated from Hebrew and adapted
by Helen Frenkley

Neot Kedumim
The Biblical Landscape Reserve in Israel

Typeset by Total Graphics Ltd., Tel Aviv
Color separations by Scanli Ltd., Tel Aviv
Plates by Imago Ltd., Givatayim
Printing by Peli Printing Works Ltd., Givatayim
Printed in Israel

To Martin Abelove, who continues to make it possible

ALL PROCEEDS BENEFIT NEOT KEDUMIM – THE BIBLICAL LANDCAPE RESERVE IN ISRAEL

Table of Contents

Translator's Note

This is the third book by Nogah Hareuveni that I have had the privilege to translate and adapt for the English reader. It is by far the most difficult, because its main theme is contingent on the elucidation of specific Hebrew word roots that heretofore have been little understood in Hebrew and totally misunderstood in translation. From the start it was clear that no existing English translations of the Bible would help resolve these specific problems. Although the basic verses were taken from *A New Translation of the Holy Scriptures* (The Jewish Publication Society, Philadelphia, 1985), and to a lesser degree, *The New English Bible* (Oxford University Press, New York, 1971), many of the final translations were carefully worked out with the author, Nogah Hareuveni, to convey his understanding of the intricacies and meaning of the language of the Hebrew Scriptures. The one exception is the twenty-third psalm, whose verses embody the essential theme of this book, and which we felt was too well known in its King James version to be reworded for accuracy of translation. Where necessary, the more accurate translations are explained in the body of the author's text. Throughout this book, chapter and verse numbers are those of the traditional Masoretic [1] Hebrew Bible; readers may find discrepancies with familiar English Bibles, primarily in verse numbers.

The accepted conventions are used to indicate quotations from the Mishnah (name of tractate, followed by chapter and paragraph number), the Babylonian Talmud (name of tractate, number of the leaf, followed by "a" or "b" to indicate the page side that is standard to all editions of the Babylonian Talmud), and the Jerusalem Talmud (always indicated as such) followed by the tractate, chapter, and paragraph number. Brief information is given in the margins on those Talmudic Sages mentioned in the text.

I have employed the alternate scholarly designations BCE ("Before the Common Era") and CE ("Common Era") for BC and AD.

Helen Frenkley

1. **Masoretic** (lit., traditional) **text** — the work that extended through the Talmudic period and ended about the eighth century CE, whose purpose, both oral and written, was the precise preservation of the holy text. It emerged as the authoritative text of the Hebrew Scriptures and determined the voweling. (The Hebrew alphabet has only consonants.) It also established the order of the 39 books of the Hebrew Scriptures and the division of the texts into sections (chapters) and weekly portions (for the weekly recitations in synagogues).

A Personal Word to the Reader

This is the third volume in the ***Biblical Heritage*** series published by Neot Kedumim. The first book, ***Nature in Our Biblical Heritage*** (1980), deals with the Biblical descriptions of the Land of Israel and the holidays of Israel and how these are rooted in the realities of nature of the Land of Israel — how the Land of Israel and the Biblical heritage are indivisible. ***Tree and Shrub in Our Biblical Heritage*** (1984) deals with individual plants of Israel that are central to specific Biblical and Talmudic accounts and imagery. The present volume, ***Desert and Shepherd in Our Biblical Heritage***, deals with very few plants and not a single holiday. Still it is a natural sequel to the previous two books. It continues the theme I have spent my life demonstrating: the necessity of intimacy with Israel's nature and landscape to understand the wellspring of the Bible and its gifts to the world.

The many photographs in this book are intended to produce in the reader at least part of the effect on me that the desert has had — and continues to have — during my hikes in the Judean Desert, in the open spaces of the Negev, and in the mountains of Sinai, from before the creation of the State of Israel till today. [1] The impressions of those early years of hiking in these deserts produced ***New Light on the Book of Jeremiah***, published 40 years ago in Hebrew by Am Oved. From then, through the period of desert training with the Palmach [2] in the early 1940's to the writing of this book in 1990, these rich impressions and experiences have continued to accumulate. Suddenly another verse springs from between the desert crags, and a new insight materializes for me while I plunge into a deep water-filled rock cavity, or when I photograph hikers taking refuge from the oppressive heat, sunk in sleep while protected by "the shade of a massive rock in an exhausted land." (Isaiah 32:2)

Over the years I have been repeatedly asked by hikers, guides, students, and teachers of Bible and Land-of-Israel studies to publish a new edition of ***New Light on the Book of***

1. Most of the photographs in this book have been incorporated as integral parts of the text and therefore, with a few exceptions, are not captioned.

2. Palmach — the permanently mobilized striking force of the Haganah. **Haganah** — the underground military organization of the Jewish settlers of Eretz Yisrael from 1920 to 1948 (during the British Mandate over Palestine). With the declaration of the State of Israel, it became the Israel Defense Forces (IDF).

7

3. Sages – the spiritual-religious leaders and teachers of the Jewish people for a thousand years, from the time of the rebuilding of the Second Temple (520 BCE) to the completion of the Babylonian Talmud in the late fifth century CE. The Sages of the Mishnah and the Gemara (see marginal note 4) are collectively called the Talmudic Sages. The title "rabbi" or "rabban" is given to all the Mishnaic Sages (the *tannaim* תנאים) and to those Sages of the Gemara (the *amoraim* אמוראים) who resided in Israel. The title "rav" or the absence of a prefix before the name indicates the *amoraim* of the Babylonian Talmud. Usually information on *tannaim* and *amoraim* includes the chronological order of the "generations" in which they acquired the status of rabbinic authority.

Jeremiah. I have attempted to respond to these requests by incorporating into this volume most of the ideas I presented in that book. However, with a few exceptions, I did not include portions that dealt with "higher Biblical criticism" by commentators far removed from Israel. Forty years ago it was important to present their ideas to show that when the prophet's immediate surroundings – the landscapes and vistas – are unfamiliar, it is impossible to understand his personality and style. This unawareness led remote Biblical critics to devote much effort to "clarifying" the "confusions of the original text." To everyone's relief, during the past decades the centrality of the environmental context has become accepted in most scholarly Biblical circles, at least here in Israel.

During these intervening years many books and articles have been published in Israel, the result of detailed research conducted in the Judean, Negev, and Sinai deserts and the borderline desert regions. A number of these publications include an effort to understand the Bible and the Sages [3] on the basis of familiarity with the desert and life in it. Relying on the wise advice of Solomon, "One further warning, my son, beware of writing endless books..." (Ecclesiastes 12:12), I have tried to minimize background material that can be found in other publications. On the other hand, I have tried to emphasize those concepts that, to the best of my knowledge, have not been dealt with in any of this wealth of material. It is possible, however, that some of the ideas presented here have, unknown to me, already appeared in print. I will be grateful to readers who call my attention to any such instance so that it may be properly credited in subsequent editions.

To make this book accessible to as wide an audience as possible, I have refrained from giving it the form of a scientific treatise, despite its firm basis in scientific method and research. To help the reader, the text is arranged in two unequal columns. The wide column deals with subjects that are connected by associative links and may be read as a single narration. The narrow column offers supplementary information that emanates from the main wide-columned text.

This book was read in Hebrew manuscript by **Shlomo**

Teitlebaum, **Arie Salomon**, **Yonathan Frenkel**, and **Nirit Kreiman**, senior staff members of Neot Kedumim — The Biblical Landscape Reserve in Israel, and by **Dalit Shiloni**, a past guide at Neot Kedumim. They all made significant comments and contributions based on their particular spheres of interest and their long experience guiding many thousands of visitors of all ages at Neot Kedumim.

The English version of this book was written by **Helen Frenkley**, my associate at Neot Kedumim for the past 21 years, who has been my faithful partner in the development of all the educational and administrative aspects of this project. Because of her familiarity with the material, Helen was able to do much more than translate the text. She took on the formidable task of making the contents understandable to readers not steeped in the Bible or Talmud.[4] In addition, she played a major role in the selection of photographs from among thousands of slides, most of which I took during my trips to the areas described in the book.

The polishing of the English version of this book was

4. Talmud — "Just as the Bible is the foundation of Judaism, the Talmud is the central pillar supporting the entire spiritual and intellectual edifice of Jewish life. The Talmud, in the broader sense of the term, is made up of two components: the **Mishnah**, which is the first written summary of the Oral Law, and the **Gemara** (called Talmud in the more restricted sense of the term), which is formally an explanation of and commentary on the Mishnah... The Mishnah consists of six orders (*sedarim*

סדרים), further divided into 63 tractates (*masekhet* מסכת, pl. *masakhtot* מסכתות). Since the Mishnah was at first transmitted orally and thus had to be committed to memory, its Hebrew style is very terse. Much of the Mishnah would defy understanding without the vast commentary that is called the Gemara. For three centuries (c.200-500 CE) after the compilation and editing of the Mishnah, the rabbis and their students discussed and analyzed the Mishnah. Their questions, discussions, and solutions make up the Talmud [Gemara]." (*The Reference Guide* to the *Steinsaltz Edition* of the *Talmud*, Random House, New York, 1989, pp. 1,2) After the destruction of the Second Temple in 70 CE, two main centers existed for the study of the Mishnah: Israel and Babylon. As a result, two distinct Talmuds emerged: that of Israel, called the Jerusalem Talmud, and the second, the Babylonian Talmud.

accomplished thanks to the dedicated services of what we by now consider our "regular" team of editors: **Natalie Frenkley**, research analyst and editor, **Alex Frenkley**, past deputy director of the Russian division of the Voice of America, **Lillian Steinfeld**, experienced copy editor, **Paul Steinfeld**, forest manager in upstate New York, who also has faithfully served as secretary-treasurer of American Friends of Neot Kedumim, and **Abe Schechter** — all devoted friends of Neot Kedumim. The all-important proofreading of the text was done by **Beth Steinfeld Uval** of Jerusalem.

The graphic design of this volume is patterned on the first two books in this series; in all three I was assisted by **Helen Frenkley** and guided by my friend, the graphic designer **Zvi Narkiss**. The layout of the pictures and text in this volume was primarily done with infinite patience by my son, **Ma'ayan Hareuveni** (also a member of the Neot Kedumim staff), who forced the Macintosh IICi computer to succumb to his difficult demands even in the wee morning hours. The original slides were converted into printed pictures for the computer's scanner by our staffer **Arie Reisman**.

My gratitude to all these, without whose inestimable help this volume could not have seen the light of day in its present form.

My particular thanks to the Honorable Fifth President of the State of Israel, Knesset Member **Yitzhak Navon**, Chairman of Neot Kedumim, who gave me no rest until he saw the manuscripts in Hebrew and English.

I extend my earnest gratitude to **Dr. Dov Goldberger**, whose enthusiastic and fruitful efforts to put Neot Kedumim on the map enabled me to take the time to write and publish this book.

Without my wife, **Drora Hareuveni**, who encouraged and drove me forward each step of the way, this book would have taken infinitely longer to write, and for this she has my most special gratitude.

It is impossible to end these personal words of acknowledgment without telling the reader about that incomparable individual, **Martin Abelove**, to whom the previous two volumes are dedicated, and to whom this volume is hereby presented with love and admiration. Martin Abelove's uniqueness lies in the way he extends his support. He never needs to be asked; Martin initiates his support after careful and quiet verification, when he is convinced it will further his goal of improving the quality and content of Jewish education.

Martin became involved with us when Neot Kedumim was still in its earliest stages in the then barren, dry environs of the Modi'in region of Israel. When he heard of the dream to establish an extensive network of Biblical and Talmudic gardens encapsulating the nature and landscapes of the country, he made every effort to grasp its potential impact on Jewish education in Israel and abroad. He intuitively felt, even then, that Neot Kedumim has a distinctive role in explaining the common ground of all Jews − the Land of Israel − and decided to do everything in his power to set Neot Kedumim on its feet. He said not a word of his intentions to anyone involved with the project. He checked and probed, asked endless questions, and finally concluded that he had to make a major and unique contribution. He suggested providing the means to enable us to publish a series of richly illustrated books that would open to the reader the literal as well as figurative roots of the Land of Israel in the Bible and in the words of the Sages. With extraordinary generosity Martin Abelove provided the tools with which we began the serious development of all of Neot Kedumim.

Truly Neot Kedumim is blessed to have such friends involved in its development.

Nogah Hareuveni
Neot Kedumim, 1991

Introduction

A Psalm of David.

"The Lord is my shepherd; I shall not want.
He maketh me to lie down in green pastures;
He leadeth me beside the still waters.
He restoreth my soul;
He leadeth me in the paths of righteousness for
His name's sake.

Yea, though I walk through the valley of the
shadow of death,
I will fear no evil, for Thou art with me.
Thy rod and Thy staff they comfort me.

Thou preparest a table before me in the presence of
mine enemies;
Thou anointest my head with oil;
My cup runneth over.
Surely goodness and mercy shall follow me
all the days of my life,
And I will dwell in the house of the Lord forever."

(Psalm 23) (King James translation)

The sense of deep peace and assurance psalm 23 evokes makes it one of the best-loved of the psalms, recited the world over by millions of people, Christians and Jews. **So why did I choose in this book — ostensibly dealing with the harsh, dry desert in whose every corner lurks danger — to begin with this particular psalm, which portrays "green pastures," "still waters," "paths of righteousness," and "comfort"?**

The title of each chapter is a verse from psalm 23. Using this device I have tried to convey the extent to which this psalm encapsulates the experiences and feelings of David, the young shepherd, during his wandering in the desert. The psalm was an instrument through which the poet expressed the memories and hopes of the entire nation.

"Now Moses, tending the flock of his father-in-law Jethro, the priest of Midian, drove the flock into the wilderness. (Exodus 3:1) Rabbi Yehoshua [1] said: Why did he go with them to the wilderness? Because he foresaw that the Israelites would be elevated from the wilderness, as it is said: Who is she that comes up out of the desert? (Song of Songs. 3:6) For from the desert they had manna, the quails, the well, the Tabernacle, the Holy Presence, the priesthood, (and) the kingdom..."(Shmot Rabbah 2,4)

"Who is she that comes up out of the desert? (Song of Songs 3:6, 8:5) Israel's elevation is from the desert; her division [into the twelve tribes] is from the desert...The Torah [2] came from the desert, the Tabernacle from the desert, the Sanhedrin [3] from the desert, the priesthood from the desert, the service of the Levites from the desert, the kingdom from the desert [all these were instituted or promulgated in the desert]...and all the excellent gifts that God bestowed on Israel came from the desert." (Shir HaShirim Rabbah 3, 5)

These homilies of the Talmudic Sages express a collective national experience, transmitted from generation to generation. It was a lengthy process to transform the Israelites from a society of slaves — whose lives were dictated by their oppressors — to an independent and ordered nation with its own leadership and laws, and the aspiration for the national development in the land of its forefathers. The process began in the deserts of Sinai and the southern Negev, where it evolved for many years while the nation adjusted to desert life.

"Who is she that comes up out of the desert?" The answer is she who "leans upon her beloved." (8:5) The attitude of the Sages, that these words describe the elevation — or ascent — of the "daughter of Israel" from the desert to the Promised Land, is a direct continuation of the prophetic tradition passed down to the Sages over the intervening centuries. The prophets of Israel compared the relationship between the people and their God to the relationship between two lovers, with its ups and downs, periods of closeness and tenderness as well as of anger and dissent. In those distant days, immediately following the exodus from Egypt, this relationship was strained by the many hardships that beset the people during their wandering in the desert, as is reflected in Moses' words to the people:

1. Rabbi Yehoshua (ben Hananya) − third generation *tanna* (80-110 CE) who served in the Temple at the time of its destruction. After the destruction of the Temple he headed a court of law *(bet din)* in Peki'in (in the Galilee) and participated in a number of missions to Rome where he debated with the Emperor Hadrian.

2. Torah — the Pentateuch, the five books of Moses.

3. Sanhedrin − the supreme political, religious, and judicial body in Israel, especially during the Roman period, both before and after the destruction of the Second Temple, until about 425 CE; also known as the Great Assembly.

"Remember, never forget, how you provoked the Lord your God to anger in the desert: from the day that you left the land of Egypt until you reached this place, you have continued defiant toward the Lord."

(Deuteronomy 9:7)

However, the period referred to by Moses in the book of Deuteronomy appears in a totally different light to the prophet Jeremiah:

"I accounted to your favor the devotion of your youth, your love as a bride when you followed Me in the wilderness, in a land not sown." (Jeremiah 2:2)

In contrast to that "honeymoon" period in the desert, which Jeremiah saw as the nation's "devotion of youth," his own time seemed to be the source of all evil, from which one could flee only to the desert:

"Oh, to be in the desert, at an encampment for wayfarers! Oh, to leave my people, to go away from them [4] — for they are all adulterers, a band of traitors."

(Jeremiah 9:1)

The centuries between the wandering in Sinai and the period of Jeremiah saw many changes overtake the people of Israel — primarily the evolution from tribes of nomadic shepherds to a nation of farmers. This cardinal change caused an upheaval which endangered the faith in one God and shook moral principles. The first book in this series, *Nature in Our Biblical Heritage* (Neot Kedumim, 1980), deals with this phenomenon and discusses how the Bible fought against the "temptation to serve other gods." (Deuteronomy 11:16)

I hope this book will steep the reader in the landscapes of the desert and so enable understanding of the contradictory feelings that this harsh and challenging region evoked in the Bible and in the writings of the Sages. I would like to share my conviction that the desert in Biblical sources cannot be understood without seeing it also as pastureland. I hope the reader will also understand how it happened that the shepherd did not become despised; the shepherd was not considered inferior to the farmer even after the great majority of the nation

4. The desert as a place of refuge

Jeremiah was not the only one who saw the desert as a place of refuge from the noisy throngs. The prophet Elijah, Simon the Hashmonean, John the Baptist, and Jesus of Nazareth all spent periods of time in the Judean Desert. Throughout history, the deserts of Judea and Benjamin served as places of asylum for deserters, revolutionaries, and for sects who veered from the mainstream. Many groups that found shelter in this region left their mark upon it: the Essenes and other Dead Sea sects left behind the Dead Sea Scrolls; Bar Kokhba and his forces, letters relating to their daily life during the Great Revolt against Rome (132-135 CE); between the fourth and seventh centuries, many Christian hermits and monks found spiritual refuge here. Several of the monasteries built during that period, such as the Monastery of Mar Saba in Nahal Kidron and the Monastery of St. George in Nahal Prat, are still functioning today, maintained by a handful of dedicated monks.

earned their living as tillers of soil. On the contrary, the Bible frequently presents the shepherd as a symbol of the ideal leader, as a model for the king himself, and even speaks of God as the Shepherd of His people.

Chapter I

" The Lord is my shepherd,
I shall not want. " (Psalm 23:1)

Northern end of the Dead Sea and the "plain of the Jordan" as seen from the Judean Desert.

Shepherds and farmers

"We your servants are shepherds, as were also our fathers." (Genesis 47:3)

This declaration of their occupation by Jacob's sons to Pharaoh is amply confirmed in the stories of the patriarchs. According to Genesis, it is clear that from their first entry into the Promised Land the forefathers of the nation of Israel were shepherds. The names of the first stops on Abraham's journey in the hilly regions (the **"oaks of Moreh"** near Shechem [Nablus] (Genesis 12:6) and **"the oaks of Mamre"** in Hebron (Genesis 13:18)) indicate that the places he chose to sojourn were forested areas, identified by the predominant oak trees.

Abraham, who was "very rich in cattle" (Genesis 13:2), avoided entering the cultivated areas farmed by the Canaanites in the valleys and plains. This is emphasized in the Bible: "The Canaanites were then in the land." (Genesis 12:6) and "The Canaanites and Perizzites were then dwelling in the land." (Genesis 13:7) But the main emphasis of the story in chapter 13 of Genesis is the importance of delineating clear boundaries not only between grazing land and farmland, but also among grazing lands allotted to different flocks. Years of shepherding experience taught the patriarchs the dangers of overgrazing, which can utterly destroy all available pastureland.

"And there was quarreling between Abram's herdsmen and Lot's.[1] — The Canaanites and Perizzites were then dwelling in the land. — Abram said to Lot: Let there be no strife between you and me, between my herdsmen and yours, for we are kinsmen. Is not the whole land before you? Let us separate: if you go north, I will go south; and if you go south, I will go north. Lot looked about him and saw how well watered was the whole plain of the Jordan, all of it — this was before the Lord had destroyed Sodom and Gomorrah — all the way to Zoar, like the garden of the Lord, like the land of Egypt. So Lot chose for himself the whole plain of the Jordan, and Lot journeyed eastward. Thus

1. Why did they quarrel?

"Why did they quarrel with each other? ...The shepherds would take Abraham's herds out to graze muzzled so they would not damage property, while Lot's flocks were not muzzled. Abraham's shepherds quarreled with Lot's shepherds, saying to them: Why do you give Lot a bad name by taking out his herds unmuzzled...?" (Psikta Rabbati, 3, 3, in the name of Rabbi Hiyya bar Abba)

According to this story, it seems that in the period of Rabbi Hiyya bar Abba, the end of the third and early fourth century CE, there was a practice of driving flocks to pasture with their mouths muzzled to prevent them from damaging fields and orchards on the way to grazing land. The muzzles were, of course, removed when the flock reached suitable pasture.

Mount Sodom reflected in the southern end of the Dead Sea.

2. "Pitching his tents all the way to Sodom"

These verses give an extraordinary glimpse of lush grazing land that stretched over a huge area in the vicinity of the Dead Sea. Clearly the "plain of the Jordan" that Lot saw is the area to the north of the Dead Sea. This is evident not only from the fact that the mouth of the Jordan River is at the northern end of the Dead Sea, but also because of Lot's vantage point — Bethel, in the hilly region later allotted to the tribe of Benjamin. In this region there are several points from which the northern part of the Dead Sea and the mouth of the Jordan River are visible, but not the southern part or the region of Sodom. From the description "all of it (was well watered) **before** the Lord had destroyed Sodom and Gomorrah" it is evident that this was written **after** the aforesaid destruction, at a time when the condition of the northern plain of the Jordan was as arid as that of the southern region. The continuation of the story in Genesis 13 indicates that the grazing areas chosen by Lot stretched from the plain of Jordan all the way to Sodom. Today, this story

they parted from each other; Abram remained in the land of Canaan, while Lot settled in the cities of the Plain, **pitching his tents all the way to Sodom.** [2] (Genesis 13:7-12)

"All shepherds are an abomination to the Egyptians."

While the story of Abraham and Lot shows the need to allocate different grazing areas in the Land of Israel, the story of Joseph hints at the **stringent separation** in Egypt **between grazing and farming areas**. This part of Egypt that was "well watered...like the garden of the Lord" (Genesis 13:10) was, of course, mostly arable land. It was irrigated by channels that carried water from the Nile River to the cultivated fields. Shepherds were permitted to pasture their flocks only in those areas where the higher soil salinity rendered the land unsuitable for cultivation. When famine overtook the Land of Israel during the time of Jacob, he and his sons went down to Egypt with all their flocks. This could have provoked dangerous confrontation with the Egyptians. So Joseph instructed his brothers before their meeting with Pharaoh:

> "When Pharaoh summons you and asks: What is your occupation? You shall answer: We have been herdsmen all our lives, as our fathers were before us, in order that you be allowed to dwell in the land of Goshen. **For all shepherds are an abomination to the Egyptians.**" (Genesis 46:33-34)

Joseph won Pharaoh's permission to settle his father and brothers in Egypt, **despite the fact that they were shepherds**, on condition that they limit themselves to the grazing area known as the "land of Goshen" — an area completely separated from cultivated fields. Centuries later, during the attempted revolt against Moses in Sinai, Dathan and Abiram longingly dub the land of Goshen "the land flowing with milk and honey" (Numbers 16:13), applying the exact words used earlier by the scouts sent out by Moses to describe the Land of Israel (Numbers 13:27) after they saw its forest-covered hills and slopes — every shepherd's ideal.

The changing levels of the Dead Sea leave their mark on the shoreline.   **opposite page**: *"Lot's wife" - a salt formation at Mount Sodom*

When they left Egypt, the Children of Israel took with them "cattle in great numbers, both flocks and herds" (Exodus 12:38) and they kept to the shepherding occupation of their forebears during the years of wandering in Sinai and the Negev, as affirmed in the book of Numbers (14:33): **"your children (shall) herd in the desert for forty years."**

The shepherd and his flock; the plowman and his team

It might be supposed that after the entry into the Promised Land, with the clearing of the forestland and the transformation of wild "milk and honey" areas to groves of fruit trees and vineyard-covered terraces [see *Nature in Our Biblical Heritage*, Neot Kedumim, 1980], and with the radical changes in life-style that followed these upheavals, the status of the shepherd in the restructured society would rapidly sink and that the shepherd would even be considered an "abomination," as he was in Egypt. But **the status of the shepherd and of grazing did not change in Israel**, at least not during the 700 years between the entry into the Promised Land with Joshua and the destruction of the First Temple in 587 BCE. In fact, **the occupation of the shepherd was considered so important and honorable that it became the symbol of ideal leadership**. The reason can be found in **the unique geography of Israel, where desert regions lie in close proximity to cultivated areas.** This enabled shepherds to continue grazing their flocks in the desert without trespassing on the farmland that developed all through the mountainous areas of Judea. In every settlement straddling the boundary of the mountains and the desert, shepherd and farmer coexisted. Mixed farmholds were common: the youngsters led the herds to pasture in the desert while the adults farmed the land around the settlement. (3)

A clear reflection of this is found in the words of Jeremiah, who was from Anatot (Jeremiah 1:1), a village a few miles northeast of Jerusalem, lying between the hill country of the tribe of Benjamin to the west and the desert descending to the Dead Sea to the east. To Jeremiah, the peaceful pairing of

sounds unbelievable, because the shores of the Dead Sea are notoriously inhospitable: terribly hot, highly salty, with very little vegetation. But this Biblical description can be accepted if the reader is aware that even in historical (as opposed to geological) times, the level of the Dead Sea underwent radical changes. These variations resulted in dramatic shifts, especially in the southern half of the Dead Sea, but its effect on the shoreline also had a strong impact on the northern section.

Hikers in this area are familiar with the "P.E.F. rock" located at the foot of Rosh Tzukim ("Rosh Feshkha") just alongside the road skirting the Dead Sea between Aynot Tzukim and Nahal Kidron. This road was built in 1970, on artificial landfill. Before then, the rock was at the waterline. Between 1900 and 1913, the British physician Masterman annually marked the fluctuating water levels of the Dead Sea on this rock on behalf of the Palestine Exploration Fund.

Joseph Braslavi (1896-1972), a pioneer Israeli geographer (in his book, *Round and Round the Dead Sea,* part of his six-volume series *Do You Know the Land?*,

19

Hakibbutz Hameuhad, Tel Aviv, 1956, p. 32), described the evidence around the perimeter of the Dead Sea that during periods of low water levels, large sections of its shore were dry. In every place where such an exposed area was at the mouth of a wadi emanating from the mountains, along both shores of the sea, the salt leached out of the soil and rich grazing vegetation sprang up. As the Bible in fact attests, the story recounted in Genesis of the battle of the "four kings against the five" that broke out when Lot was in Sodom took place "at the Valley of Siddim, **now** the Dead Sea" (Genesis 14:3), and "the Valley of Siddim was dotted with asphalt pits" (Genesis 14:10). Obviously, in that period the Dead Sea was at such a low

farmer and shepherd was so natural that in his angriest prophecy against Babylon — in which he describes the total destruction of all ordered life — Jeremiah cries out:

"I will smash your [Babylon's] **shepherd and flock,** I will smash your **plowman and team**...So will I repay Babylon and the people of Chaldea for all the wicked things they did to Zion before your eyes — declares the Lord."

(Jeremiah 51:23-25)

And in his prophecy of the good days that will come to Israel with the return to Zion from Babylonian exile:

"He who scattered Israel will gather them, and will **guard them as a shepherd his flock**...They shall come and sing on the heights of Zion, radiant over the bounty of the Lord — **over grain and**

wine and oil, and over sheep and cattle. Their soul shall become like a watered garden and they shall never sorrow again." (Jeremiah 31:10-11)

And similarly:

> "**Farmers and shepherds who wander with the flocks shall live together in** Judah and all its towns." (Jeremiah 31:23)

However, when Jeremiah becomes angry with the sins of the people, he gives vent to the wish that grazing areas encroach on arable lands, prophesying that these will spread to the hilly farming areas:

> "Thus said the Lord of Hosts: in this ruined place, without man and cattle, and in all its towns, **there shall be a pasture for shepherds, where they can rest their flocks: in the towns of the hill country, in the towns of the plain, and in the towns of the Negev, in the land of Benjamin and in the environs of Jerusalem and in the towns of Judah**, sheep shall pass under the shepherd's hands as he counts them." (Jeremiah 33:12-13)

The preference for shepherding in Israel was not only a consequence of Jeremiah's own way of life. He strove to return the people to the simpler shepherding life because the difficulties intrinsic in raising crops in Israel constantly tempted the farmer to turn to the idol worship of the Canaanite farmers and thus to break away from the belief in one God.[4] This, seemingly, was also the background for the lesson in faithfulness by the sons of Jonadab ben-Rechab that Jeremiah holds up for the people to emulate:

> "The word that came to Jeremiah from the Lord... Go to the house of Rechab and speak to them and bring them to the House of the Lord, to one of the chambers, and give them wine to drink. So I took Jaazaniah son of Jeremiah son of Habaziniah, and his brothers, all his sons, and the whole household of Rechab; and I brought

level that its entire southern seabed was exposed. So clearly in the time of Lot the entire region surrounding the Dead Sea was dotted with stretches of green grazing land, exactly as stated in Genesis: "like the garden of the Lord, like the land of Egypt." Also, in such a period of low water level, the Jordan River delta is greatly expanded and the grazing areas of the "plain of the Jordan" are enlarged.

The comparison of the plain of the Jordan of that period to the land of Egypt, whose delta region was so abundantly watered by the inundation of the Nile, depicts the impressive grazing lands chosen by Lot.

3. "Many shepherds have destroyed My vineyard"

As opposed to the peaceful coexistence between shepherd and farmer living on the desert borderland, the Bible gives ample evidence of destructive incursions by shepherds from the east. For example in the days of Gideon: "After the Israelites had done their sowing, Midian, Amalek, and the Kedemites would come up and raid them; they would attack them, **destroy the produce of the land** [by grazing their flocks] all the way to Gaza, and leave no means of sustenance in Israel, not a sheep or an ox or an ass. For **they would come up with their livestock and their tents, swarming as thick as locusts; they and their camels were innumerable. Thus they would invade the land and ravage it.** Israel was reduced to utter misery by the Midianites..." (Judges 6:3-6)

Jeremiah prophesied God's punishment of Israel not only in the guise of conquest by Babylon, but also through the incursion of peoples from the east who would take advantage of the appropriate moment during the siege of Judah. The description of this punishment is so vibrant that it could have been written only by someone who himself had lived on the edge of the desert and had personally experienced such an invasion, or, at the very least, had heard graphic tales of the raiders likely to appear in time of upheaval: **"Many shepherds have destroyed My vineyard**, have trampled My field, have made My delightful field a desert wasteland." (Jeremiah 12:10) But Jeremiah's description is incomplete without the depiction of the catastrophe that will overwhelm the shepherds themselves in the desert: **"Plunderers have come upon all the bare hills of the desert**, a sword of the Lord devouring the land from one end to the other; no creature is safe." (Jeremiah 12:12)

Even in his famous description of the evil and disaster that will "come from the north" (Jeremiah 4:5-17), Jeremiah uses one of the catastrophes facing shepherds as a metaphor for the calamity which will befall the nation: "Disaster overtakes disaster, for all the land has been ravaged. **Suddenly my tents have been ravaged, in a moment, my tent cloths (are destroyed)."** (Jeremiah 4:20) And also, **"My tents are ravaged, all my tent cords are broken.** My children have gone and are no more; **no one is left to stretch out my tents and hang my tent cloths."** (Jeremiah 10:20)

Even in the prophecy of the disaster that shall "go forth from nation to nation; a great storm unleashed from the remotest parts of earth" (Jeremiah 25:32), the vengeance of God against the nations who warred against Israel is seen by Jeremiah as the catastrophe that befalls the shepherd: "Howl, shepherds, and cry aloud, strew [dust] on yourselves,

them to the House of the Lord...I set bowls full of wine and cups before the men of the house of the Rechabites, and said to them: Have some wine.

"They replied: We will not drink wine, for our forefather, Jonadab ben-Rechab, commanded us: You shall never drink wine, either you or your children. **Nor shall you build houses or sow fields, or plant vineyards, nor shall you own such things; but you shall live in tents all your days, so that you may live long upon the land where you sojourn.** And we have obeyed our forefather Jonadab ben-Rechab in all that he commanded us: we never drink wine, neither we nor our wives nor our sons and daughters. Nor do we build houses to live in, and **we do not own vineyards or fields for sowing; but we live in tents.** We have obeyed and done all that our forefather Jonadab commanded us...

"Then the word of the Lord came to Jeremiah...Go say to the men of Judah and the inhabitants of Jerusalem: Learn the lesson of obeying My commands...Turn back, every one of you, from your wicked ways and mend your deeds; do not follow other gods to serve them that you may remain on the land that I gave to you and your fathers. But you did not listen to Me. The family of Jonadab ben-Rechab have indeed fulfilled the charge that their forefather gave them; but this people has not listened to Me."

(Jeremiah 35:1-10, 12-13, 15-16)

Shlomo Teitlebaum, a senior staff member of Neot Kedumim, himself a grape grower in Moshav Kfar Truman, noted that this injunction against drinking wine was not a vow of abstinence but a direct consequence of the prohibition against working the land and cultivating vineyards. This analysis is further confirmed by another ban laid on the household of Rechab: not to build permanent dwellings but to live in tents. **As tent dwellers, abstaining from all tilling of the**

soil, they could only be shepherds. This understanding of the tradition passed down in the Rechab family, says Shlomo Teitlebaum, clarifies why Jeremiah sees in it the model of excellence for the entire nation. As mentioned above, the "following of other gods to serve them" occurred primarily because of the change from shepherding to farming. It appears, therefore, that the Rechab family not only was faithful to its forefather but, consequently, also remained true to the belief in one God.

That same conviction and longing is voiced in Jeremiah's words:

> "I accounted to your favor the devotion of your youth, your love as a bride, when you followed Me in the desert, in a land not sown." [5]
>
> (Jeremiah 2:2)

Sown fields on the threshold of the Judean Desert facing "a land not sown."

you masters of the flock! It is your turn to go to the slaughter, and you shall fall like fine rams. The shepherds shall have nowhere to flee, the herdsmen, no way of escape. Hark, the shepherds cry out, the herdsmen howl, for the Lord is ravaging their flock, and their peaceful pastures lie in ruins beneath His anger." (Jeremiah 25:34-36)

4. "Lest you be lured away"
In *Nature In Our Biblical Heritage* (Neot Kedumim, 1980) I described the special problems involved in raising each one of the "seven varieties" by which Moses described the Promised Land to the Children of Israel during their wandering in the Sinai Desert. ("A land of wheat and barley, of grapes, figs and pomegranates, a land of olive oil and [date] honey." Deuteronomy 8:8) The Israelites who changed from nomadic shepherds in the desert to settled farmers were tempted to adopt the idol-worshipping practices of the Canaanite farmer as "insurance" against the uncertainties inherent in raising these crops in the Land of Israel. During the entire First Temple period, the prophets fought against this practice, but idol worship ceased in Israel only with the building of the Second Temple, some 800 years after the entry into the Promised Land.

5. "A land not sown"
Jeremiah gives an interesting definition of the term desert: "a land not sown." (2:2) Its full power can be felt today only if you stand atop one of the hills on the edge of the Judean Desert on a rainy winter day and cast your eye in the direction of the Dead Sea. At your feet, you see fields of fresh, green grain stretching towards the east. Farther off, the worn, whitish-yellow hills form a barrier beyond which the fields do not continue. From the village of Anatot,

Jeremiah's birthplace, the eye can see, one or two kilometers east of the desert's threshold, an isolated green patch of sown ground that, because of its topographical location and soil composition, is able to absorb enough water to sustain a crop. These green pockets are especially conspicuous because they are in such sharp contrast to the surrounding barren hills of the Judean Desert. Since childhood, this scenery formed part of Jeremiah's familiar world. His view of the desert, the "land not sown" versus the sown land, was a natural reflection of his immediate environment. He must have been familiar with each and every arable pocket-sized field, and personally aware of the dangers faced by the traveler through the "land not sown." Here, in a moment of deep compassion for his people, Jeremiah remembers the nation's "youthful love," when only the boundless love for God gave it the courage to believe in Him strongly enough to leave the green and fertile Nile delta, to follow Him for many long years in an unsown and barren land, and finally to reach the land He had promised.

6. The historical context of Jeremiah and Ezekiel

Jeremiah and Ezekiel were contemporaries living and prophesying during some of the most momentous events in Israel's history: the deportation of King Jehoiakhin in 597 BCE to Babylon with the leading citizens of Jerusalem (including Ezekiel), and the final fall of Jerusalem and the destruction of the First Temple in 587 BCE, when Nebuchadnezzar put an end to the Kingdom of Judah.

Both Ezekiel, the exiled aristocratic priest, and Jeremiah, the shepherd, recognized that the power of Babylon

In those days of young and unblemished love the people of Israel were shepherds in the desert, not yet troubled by the problems of raising crops that lured them to worship other gods.

Against this background the words of Hosea are especially striking:

> "Their mother has played the harlot. She that conceived them has acted shamelessly because she thought: I will go after my lovers who supply my bread and my water, my wool and my linen, my oil and my drink...**And she did not consider that it was I who bestowed on her the grain and wine and oil**...She went after her lovers, forgetting Me, declares the Lord.

> "Therefore, **I will woo her and lead her to the desert and speak to her tenderly.** I will give her her vineyards from there, and the Valley of Akhor as a doorway of hope. There she shall rejoice as in the days of her youth, when she came up from the land of Egypt...

> "For I will remove the names of the gods from her mouth...And I will espouse you forever: I will espouse you with righteousness and justice, and with goodness and mercy. And I will espouse you with faithfulness; then you shall be devoted to the Lord. In that day, I will respond — declares the Lord. I will respond to the sky, and it shall respond to the earth; and the earth shall respond with grain and wine and oil."

> (Hosea 2:7-8, 10, 15-17, 19-23)

These words appear to indicate that Hosea, about 200 years before Jeremiah, already saw the turning to idol worship as a consequence of the change from nomadic shepherding in the desert to an agrarian society. The temptation could be overcome only after a return to the desert, followed by a rebuilding of that settled, farming society on more faithful foundations. Such a vision is also prophesied in the words of Jeremiah concerning the future of the already-destroyed Kingdom of Israel:

"Thus said the Lord: The people that survived the sword found favor in the desert...Again you shall plant vineyards on the hills of Samaria...For the day is coming when watchmen shall proclaim on the heights of Ephraim: Come, let us go up to Zion, to the Lord our God." (Jeremiah 31:1-6)

This time, repeats Jeremiah, after the renewed affirmation in the desert of those who have survived the sword, the vineyards planted on the hills of Samaria will not lead the tribes of the north to be cut off from the Holy Temple in Jerusalem.[6] On the contrary, the watchmen [7] shall be the ones to summon the nation to come up to Jerusalem to give thanks for the bountiful crops to the one God.

Ezekiel also sees the period after exile in a similar light: pasturing herds in the desert as the first step, followed by the development of an agrarian society firmly based on an unshakeable belief in the God of Israel.

"Then I will appoint a single shepherd over them to tend them — My servant David. He shall tend them, he shall be a shepherd to them. I the Lord will be their God...And I will grant them a covenant of peace and I will banish vicious beasts from their land, **and they shall live secure in the desert, they shall sleep in the woods**...I will send down the rain in its season, rains that bring blessing. The trees of the field shall yield their fruit and the land shall yield its produce." (Ezekiel 34:23-27)

Similarly, Isaiah (about 150 years before Jeremiah and Ezekiel) sees the redemption of Israel coming only by the forced return to the shepherding life when "every place where there had been a thousand grapevines worth a thousand shekels of silver shall be covered with briars and thorns." (Isaiah 7:23)

"And in that day, each man shall save a heifer of the herd and two animals of the flock; and he shall get so much milk that he shall eat curds; for all who are left in the land shall eat [nothing but] curds and honey." (Isaiah 7:21)

was irresistible and that Judah could not hope to oppose it. Both concluded that submission to Nebuchadnezzar was the will of God, His punishment for the unfaithfulness of His people. And both believed that this punishment would bring with it contrition and eventual restoration to the homeland.

7. Border guards

The kingdom ruled by David and expanded by Solomon included at the time of the latter's death (922 BCE) all of present-day Israel and much of Syria and Jordan. Solomon's son, Rehoboam, was unable to keep the kingdom united and it split in two. The tribes living in the north (Ephraim, Manasseh, Dan, Gad, Asher, Reuben, Naftali, Issahar, and Zebulun) formed the Northern Kingdom, called the Kingdom of Israel, with its capital first in Shechem and then in Samaria. The tribes of Judah, Simon, and Benjamin maintained the continuity of King David's dynasty in the much smaller Southern Kingdom — the Kingdom of Judah.

The Northern Kingdom of Israel lasted 200 years until, in 722 BCE, it was conquered by the Assyrians, its population deported, and the land ravaged. The Southern Kingdom of Judah lasted until the destruction of Jerusalem and the Temple in 587 BCE, by Nebuchadnezzar, king of Babylon, some 700 years after the Israelites entered the Promised Land.

Perhaps Jeremiah, born about 80 years after the destruction of the Kingdom of Israel, was referring indirectly to the border guards (the "watchmen on the hills of Samaria...on the heights of Ephraim") who, according to the tradition of the Sages (Ta'anit 30b), were stationed by Jeroboam ben-Nevat, the first king of the Kingdom of Israel, to prevent the population of the Northern

In this manner grazing land shall cover Israel just as in the days when the Children of Israel entered a thickly forested land, a land "flowing with milk and honey" (a subject discussed in detail in *Nature in Our Biblical Heritage*).

The desert as pastureland

"With whom did you leave those few sheep in the desert?" (I Samuel 17:28)

What is *midbar* - מדבר?

In modern Hebrew *midbar* is used to identify arid places, with little or no rainfall, where water sources are few and far between, where there is insufficient water for crop cultivation except on a very limited scale. But a careful scanning of the

Bible and other Jewish sources shows that even though it is possible to find the word *midbar* used in this sense, in many places the word is used to convey a **grazing area**.[8] [The translator has chosen the consistent use of the word **desert** wherever *midbar* is used in the original Hebrew Biblical or Talmudic sources.] [9]

Radak [10] defines *midbar* :

"...a place to pasture the cattle is called *midbar*, whether it is close to the town or far from it." He gives this definition when examining the phrase **"in the direction of the desert"** *derekh hamidbar* דרך המדבר (Joshua 8:15), which appears in the description of Joshua's maneuver to capture the town of Ai. The desert mentioned here is close to Ai, which **is located in the hilly regions of the Judean mountains near the town of Bethel**. Therefore Radak underscores that the word *midbar* can also be used to define an area close to a town, **if it is used as a place for grazing cattle.**

While dealing with events from the days of Joshua, it is apt to quote the Sages concerning the first of the "ten stipulations" for behavior in the new Land that Joshua specified before the Children of Israel crossed the Jordan River into the Promised Land: **"that they shall graze their flocks in the thickets."** (In the *b'raita* [11] given in the Gemara, Baba Kama 81a) Joshua's stipulations, as passed on by the Sages, bring to mind another *b'raita* given in the Gemara:

"The Sages taught: **Goats and sheep** are not to be raised in the land of Israel **except in thickets of the Land of Israel**." (Baba Kama 79a)

This *b'raita* appears in the Gemara immediately after a quotation from the Mishnah on the same subject:

"Goats and sheep are not to be raised in the land of Israel, but are raised in Syria and **in the deserts of the Land of Israel**." (Baba Kama 7,7)

Both these quotations indicate a clear parallelism between the **thickets** of the *b'raita* where it is permitted to pasture cattle and the areas called **deserts** in the Mishnah.

Kingdom from going up during the pilgrimage festivals to the Temple in Jerusalem, within the boundaries of the rival Southern Kingdom, Judah.

8. Flocks are pastured in the desert.
"You led Your people like a flock in the care of Moses and Aaron. (Psalm 77:21) Why like a flock? Because as in the case of a flock no stores are gathered for it but it is fed in the desert; so the Children of Israel, during all the forty years they were in the desert, were maintained without stores. Consequently they were compared to a flock." (Bamidbar Rabbah 23,3)

9. Desert, wilderness, and wasteland
In English translations of the Hebrew Bible there is an inconsistent and indiscriminate use of both **desert** and **wilderness** for the Hebrew word *midbar*. By uniformly using the same word, desert, we hope the reader will feel the range of nuances that the Hebrew word *midbar* conveys in the Bible. By the same token, we have consistently used the word **"wilderness"** when we deemed it necessary to translate the word *arava* ערבה not as a geographical term, and **"wasteland"** for the Hebrew word *yeshimon* ישימון.

Readers interested in the definitions of *midbar* מדבר given in a number of Hebrew dictionaries based on Biblical and Talmudic sources are directed to the Hebrew original of this book, "מדבר ורועה במורשת ישראל", p.22.

10. Radak (Rabbi David Kimkhi) 1160?-1235?, Provence, France; one of the outstanding Biblical commentators and grammarians, who strove for clarity and readability in his exegesis.

11. b'raita − a legal ruling *(halakha)* of the *tannaim* in the Babylonian Talmud, not included in either the Mishnah or the Tosefta. The **Tosefta** (lit., addition) is an appendix or supplement to the Mishnah, dating from the fifth or sixth centuries CE. It contains many legal decisions that were not included in Yehudah Hanassi's redaction of the Mishnah, together with maxims and decisions frequently quoted in the Gemara. The Tosefta is divided into the same orders and tractates as the Mishnah itself, so that almost each tractate of the Mishnah has its parallel in the Tosefta.

Rashi [12] identifies the **thickets** in the *b'raita* dealing with "Joshua's stipulations" (in his clarification to the Gemara, Iruvin 17a) with the term **forest**: "They should be pastured in the **thickets** — everyone is permitted to graze his herds in the **forest** belonging to his neighbor **and the owner shall not have to give permission...**" (and similarly in the *b'raita* on the same subject in Baba Kama 81a)

This clarifies Rashi's elucidation of the "**forest of Ephraim**" mentioned in the story of the war of Absalom against David near Mahanaim, which is on the eastern bank of the Jordan River:

> "When David reached Mahanaim...the troops marched out into the open to confront the Israelites and the battle was fought in the **forest of Ephraim**...The battle spread out over that whole region, and the forest devoured more troops that day than the sword." (II Samuel 17:27, 18:6,8)

Rashi asks: "**In the forest of Ephraim**: Where was there a forest in [the land allocated to the tribe of] Ephraim on the eastern bank of the Jordan River, which was given to the tribes of Gad, Reuben, and Menasseh?" (The tribe of Ephraim was allocated land on the west, not the east, bank of the Jordan.) Rashi's answer: "Because Joshua directed that grazing shall be in the **thickets** and this is the same forest **adjacent** to the land of Ephraim but divided from it by the Jordan; **they pastured their flocks there and it was called the Forest of Ephraim.**" (Rashi on II Samuel 18:6)

We find a similar point of view in Radak's explanation:

"**In the forest of Ephraim:** How did the tribe of Ephraim come to have a forest area on the other side of the Jordan? Said the Sages: Because of the constraints imposed by Joshua, one of which was that **flocks shall be pastured in the thickets**. In other words, they were lenient about letting flocks of one tribe graze in thickets belonging to another tribe. The area allocated to Ephraim was in the land of Canaan, as is written in the book of Joshua. **Opposite their land, separated by the Jordan River, was a forest. And the tribe of Ephraim would move their flocks there** and have them graze in that forest, which was therefore called by their name, the Forest of Ephraim.'' (Radak on II Samuel 18:6)

The common denominator between desert, thicket, and forest was that all three were grazing areas because none was suitable for farming. Nevertheless, the significant difference between the desert on the one hand and the thicket and forest on the other is in the desert's minimal rainfall and consequently sparse vegetation. The desert has always been relatively unchanging, while the thicket and forest areas were cyclically cleared for agricultural land in times of peace and prosperity and reverted to forestland following wars and the resultant neglect. Because conditions in the desert did not permit farming, the changes in that landscape were minimal in comparison to the far-reaching changes that occurred − and still occur − in arable areas.

As a consequence of the repeated changes in the landscape of Israel, much of the vegetation indigenous to the hill and

12. **Rashi (Rabbi Shlomo Yitzhaki)** − lived in France and Germany in the 11th century. The most popular and authoritative commentator of all ages on the Bible and Talmud, his works became the bases for most of the subsequent traditional Biblical and Talmudic commentaries.

13. **Josephus Flavius** – first century CE Jewish historian and soldier who was an eyewitness to the destruction of the Second Temple and of Masada. His historical works are the only surviving firsthand accounts of the tumultuous events in Israel during the Roman conquest.

14. **"Do not spend the night in the *aravot* of the desert."**
The story of the tactical advice given by Hushai the Archite to David provides further proof that the term *arava* ערבה (plural, *aravot*) was used to designate various places not only south of the Dead Sea, but also north of it: "Now send at once and tell David, '**Do not**

borderland regions intermingled. Therefore the **thickets** referred to by the Sages as regions permitted for grazing, like the desert, were not limited to the borderland area. **They included all the areas in the hilly region to which agriculture did not return** and which consequently were covered again by the kind of growth that characterized the Biblical **forest**. In light of these changes in the landscape of Israel over hundreds of years, it is easier to understand the *b'raita* in the Babylonian Talmud:

"Sheep and goats are not to be raised in the land of Israel but are **permitted in the desert located in Judea and in the desert bordering Acco [Acre]."** (Baba Kama 79b) **Acco is located in the lower western Galilee, an area that today has absolutely nothing in common with a desert!**

spend the night in the *aravot* of the desert, but cross over at once**...David and all the troops with him promptly **crossed the Jordan**, and by daybreak not one was left who had not crossed the Jordan." (II Samuel 17:16, 22)

The Sharon as the *Arava*
Another well-known grazing area of Biblical times was the red sandy loam of the Sharon hills. One of the stewards

As in many places in Israel, here too major changes transpired as a result of war: "**The Galilee War**, which lasted from Nissan [April] 67 [CE] to Tishri [September] of that year [70 CE – the year of the destruction of the Second Temple], **destroyed the fertile land together with its large population and it was turned into a desert wasteland.** The books of Josephus Flavius [13] (*The Jewish War* and *The Life of Joseph*), the Talmud and the homilies convey poignant announcements of this." (Shmuel Klein, *The Land of Galilee*, Rav Kook Press, Jerusalem, 1946, p. 41)

The Rift Valley — the Arava *— a mixture* (eruv) *of green pastures and arid land*

Permission to graze sheep and goats in the lower western Galilee in the same manner as in the Judean Desert was a result of the total destruction of agriculture in this area following the Galilee War, which transformed this once-fertile area into "desert" fit only for grazing.

What is the difference between *arava* ערבה (wilderness) and *midbar* מדבר (desert)?

The Bible is replete with the name *arava* ערבה designating different areas along the Rift Valley from the Bay of Eilat in the south to the Sea of Galilee in the north.[14] Even the Dead Sea is sometimes referred to in the Bible as the ***Arava* Sea** (Deuteronomy 3:17, Joshua 3:16, and elsewhere). All places referred to as *arava* have in common a typical landscape: **a mixture (*eruv* עירוב) of fresh, verdant areas intermingled**

appointed by King David was "Shitrai the Sharonite" who was responsible for **"the cattle pasturing in Sharon"** (I Chronicles 27:29) This soil is conducive to oak trees and lush groundcover of annual flowers and perennial shrubs. The Turks were the last to destroy this natural oak forest which once covered the Sharon Valley when they cut down the trees to fuel the trains on the Cairo-Damascus railroad.

Isaiah in his description of the destruction of the Land of Israel foresees the ruin of the Sharon: "Highways are desolate, wayfarers have ceased...the land is wilted and withered; Lebanon disgraced and moldering, **Sharon is become**

with totally arid ground. This is especially obvious when the Rift is seen from the parallel mountain ranges. I believe that this striking mixture gave rise to the name of this entire Rift, ***arava*** ערבה. Among the arid areas, devoid of vegetation, the saltlands of the Arava clearly stand out: the salt that covers these surfaces permits no plant to grow. Indeed, the Bible also includes the saltlands in the Arava: "Who sets the wild horse free? Who loosens the bonds of the onager whose home I have made in the **wilderness**, the **salt land** his dwelling place?" (Job 39:5-6), and "He shall be like the

like a wilderness *(arava)* and Bashan and Carmel are stripped bare." (Isaiah 33:8,9) And conversely in his description of the resurrection of the Land, Isaiah sees the **Arava turned into the Sharon**: "The arid desert shall be glad, the wilderness *(arava)* shall rejoice...it shall receive the glory of Lebanon, the splendor of Carmel and Sharon..." (Isaiah 35:1,2)

15. "A land no man has traversed"
Jeremiah describes the trials the Children of Israel had to overcome between the exodus from Egypt and the entry into the Promised Land: "They never asked themselves: Where is the Lord who brought us up from the land of Egypt, who led us through the desert, a land of *arava* and canyons, a parched land, [a land of] the shadow of death, a land no man had traversed, where no human being

Sodom apple in the **wilderness**, which does not sense the coming of good: It is set in the scorched places of the desert, in a **salt land** without inhabitants." (Jeremiah 17:6)

We will meet the "Sodom apple in the wilderness" later. Here, I would like to call attention to the parallel between the wilderness, *arava* , and the desert, *midbar*, in these verses.[15] There are other passages in the Bible where this analogy serves to underscore how the concept of *arava* broadened over the generations to complement the descriptions of the desert.

And what is wasteland — *yeshimon* ישימון?

A similar development occurred, it seems, with the term *yeshimon*. It too appears in the Bible several times in reference to specific areas, such as the region revealed from the top of the mountains of Moab (Numbers 21:20, Deuteronomy 32:9-10), or the region to the north of the hill of Hakhakhila and the desert of Maon described in the stories of Saul's pursuit of David (I Samuel 23:19, 23:24-29). Although we do not have an exact description of the location of the *yeshimon* in Moab, the location of *yeshimon* in the stories of Saul and David is given in detail.[16] It is the desolate region located east of the fertile region of Yata (evidently the Yuttah mentioned in Joshua 15:55) which spread southeast of Hebron: "David is hiding among us in the strongholds of the groves, at the hill of Hakhakhila, south of the *yeshimon*." (I Samuel 23:19) "They left at once for Ziph, ahead of Saul; David and his men were then in the **desert of Maon, in the Arava, to the south of *yeshimon***." (I Samuel 23:24) This region was evidently called *arava* because here the edge of the desert is an area of especially high contrast (mix — *ta'arovet* תערובת) between green, fertile hills and empty wasteland (*sh'mama* שממה, from the same root as *yeshimon* ישימון). In this area there was a grove of pine trees that grow easily in this kind of soil, and which provided shade for the strongholds in which David hid.

left: Red buttercups overlook the area where Saul pursued David.
lower right: Close-up of red buttercups

had dwelt?" (Jeremiah 2:6) In this description Jeremiah depicts various regions which are also part of the desert and that not only do not serve as pasture, but are dangerous merely to cross.

16. Where is the "Rock of Separation"?

"When Saul and his men came to search, David was warned of it; and he went down to the cliff and stayed in the desert of Maon. On hearing this, Saul pursued David in the desert of Maon. Saul was making his way along one side of a hill and David and his men were on the other side of the hill. While David and his men were trying desperately to get away and Saul and his followers were closing in for the capture, a runner brought a message to Saul: Come at once! The Philistines have invaded the land. So Saul called off the pursuit and turned back to face the Philistines. This is why that place is

33

called the Rock of Separation. And David went up from there and stayed in the fastness of Ein Gedi." (I Samuel 23:25-28)

This story is so exact in its description that I believe it enables us to identify the specific location where the events occurred, called "Mount Kholed" on today's maps. This hill has a sharp, knifelike ridge about one and a quarter kilometers long, with steep slopes on both sides. (See photo on previous page.) While David was on the eastern slope on his way into the wadis leading down to the Dead Sea, Saul, on the other slope, divided his force into two flanks "trying to encircle David and his men and capture them." (I Samuel 23:26) Because David's direction lay east through open country, Saul's men could have easily captured David's forces had they deployed the pincer maneuver and pinned him down from both sides of the hill. The story leaves no doubt that David was saved only because of the message that so opportunely reached Saul: "the Philistines have invaded the land."

However, *yeshimon* — wasteland — was not only the name for specific regions; the term expanded over the centuries to complement the term *midbar* — desert — especially in the poetry of the Bible:

"He found him in a desert region, in an empty howling wasteland *(yeshimon)*. He protected him, watched over him, guarded him as the pupil of His eye." (Deuteronomy 32:10)

"O God, when You went at the head of Your people, when You marched through the wasteland *(yeshimon)*, the earth trembled, the very heavens quaked before God, the Lord of Sinai, before God, the God of Israel." (Psalm 68:8-9)

"How often did they defy Him in the desert, did they grieve Him in the wasteland *(yeshimon)*!" (Psalm 78:40)

"Their greed was insatiable in the desert, they tried God's patience in the wasteland *(yeshimon)*." (Psalm 106:14)

"Some lost their way in the desert, in the wasteland *(yeshimon)*; they found no settled place. Hungry and thirsty, their soul shriveled up." (Psalm 107:4-5)

"...I will make a road through the desert, and rivers in the wasteland *(yeshimon)*. The wild beasts shall honor Me, jackals and ostriches, for I provide water in the desert, and rivers in the wasteland *(yeshimon)* to give drink to My chosen people." (Isaiah 43:19-20)

From all the above we can conclude that the term *midbar* in Hebrew — **desert** — incorporates a number of concepts: basically it identifies a **grazing area** located in regions of little rainfall that were never cultivated. However, parallel to this, the term includes two peripheral areas: On the one hand we have seen that even a region with abundant rainfall like the Lower Galilee may, under special circumstances, be called **midbar**. On the other hand, the same term may be used for totally arid regions unsuitable even for grazing or where grazing is limited to the dry wadis where the only vegetation grows. The wide latitude given to the term *midbar* reflects the changing parameters of available grazing land: expanding to cover moister areas when agriculture was destroyed, or shrinking when drought reduced the pasturelands.

Understanding the role of the desert in the Biblical heritage rests on more than a basic familiarity with the desert itself. It also requires acquaintance with the life of shepherds and flocks and an awareness of the changes in the landscapes of Israel and in the life of the people of Israel during the nation's different historical periods. Likewise, without a fundamental familiarity with the desert in all its manifestations, it is impossible to grasp the many Biblical and Talmudic descriptions, images, and symbols plucked from the life of flocks and shepherds.

17. The shepherds' battle against the wild beasts

Among the most significant qualities needed by the Israelite shepherd were courage, physical strength, and resourcefulness. Without these he could not confront the lions and bears that survived in Israel in those places where the forestland had not been cleared by the Israelites. The most famous of these regions was the "Jordan thickets" — the dense growth which covered both banks of the Jordan and had never (until recent years) been cleared for farming. There are several accounts of lions and bears in these sheltering thickets. From here the carnivores emerged to hunt their prey, frequently among the flocks grazing in the desert between the Jordan thickets and the Judean hills. The following verses provide ample evidence:

"...As a shepherd rescues from the lion's jaws two shank bones or the tip of an ear, [in like manner] shall be rescued the Israelites who dwell in Samaria..."

(Amos 3:12)

"...A lion or a young lion growls over its prey and when the shepherds gather in force against him, is not scared by their noise or cowed by their clamor..."

(Isaiah 31:4)

"It shall be as when a lion comes up out of the thickets of the Jordan against a secure pasture..."   (Jeremiah 49:19 and 50:44)

"Israel are scattered sheep, harried by lions."   (Jeremiah 50:17)

In the New Testament, Jesus describes himself as "the good shepherd" who does not flee in the face of danger to his flock:

"I am the good shepherd, who is willing to die for the sheep. When the hired man sees a wolf coming, he abandons the sheep and runs away, because he is not a shepherd and the sheep are not his.

The leader as shepherd

"He who knows how to look after sheep...shall come and tend My people." (Shmot Rabbah 2, 2)

Shepherding was considered responsible and highly honored work in Israel even hundreds of years after the majority of the nation had become tillers of soil. Spiritual and political leadership, and even the leadership of God, is described in terms of shepherd's work. It is possible that the **special respect for the shepherd and his task emanated from their setting in the desert and wilderness.** As you will see in ensuing chapters, the shepherd in these areas had to withstand extreme hardship and danger. He had to have a superb sense of orientation, be able to adapt to the special conditions of the desert, survive periods of drought and thirst, defend his flocks from two- and four-footed marauders, and throughout concern himself with each ram and ewe, each kid and lamb.[17] His animals had to be fed without encroaching on either cultivated land or the grazing areas of other flocks. Only a shepherd with all these abilities could maintain his flocks and see them thrive in the formidable conditions of the desert and the wilderness, as the following two homilies clearly illustrate:

"Here you have two great leaders tested by God by a little thing, Who then found them trustworthy, and promoted them to greatness. **He tested David with sheep, which he led through the desert, only in order to keep them from robbing** [grazing in cultivated fields]; for so Eliav says to David: With whom did you leave those few sheep in the desert? (I Samuel 17:28) This teaches us that he fulfilled the Mishnah: One must not rear sheep and goats in Eretz Yisrael (except in the desert). God said to him: You have been found trustworthy with the sheep; come, therefore, and tend My sheep, as it is said: He brought him from tending the nursing ewes. (Psalm 78:71) Similarly in the case of Moses it says: And **he drove the flock into the desert** (Exodus 3:1) **in order to keep them from despoiling** [the fields of others]. God took him to tend Israel, as it is said: You led Your people like a flock in the care of Moses [18] and Aaron. (Psalm 77:21)" (Shmot Rabbah 2,3)

"The Lord tries the righteous. (Psalm 11:5) By what does He try him? By tending flocks. He tried David through sheep and found him to be a good shepherd, as it is said: He chose David, His servant, and took him from the sheepfolds. (Psalm 78:70) Why 'from the sheepfolds' [literally, sheep restrainers], when the word is the same as 'and the rains from heaven were restrained'? (Genesis 8:2) Because he used to restrain the older sheep from going out before the younger ones, and bring the younger ones out first, so that they should graze upon the tender grass, and afterwards he allowed the old sheep to feed from the ordinary grass, and lastly, he brought out the prime, lusty sheep to eat the tougher grass. **Whereupon God said: He who knows how to look after sheep, bestowing upon each the care it deserves, shall come and tend My people**, as it says: He brought him [David] from minding the nursing ewes to tend His people Jacob, Israel, His very own. (Psalm 78:71)" (Shmot Rabbah 2, 2)

In this homily the God of Israel is seen as the owner of the flock, who "pastures" His people so long as no shepherd is found worthy of this important and formidable task. The source of this relationship is found in the writings of the prophets that are rooted in the tradition of the patriarchs who were themselves shepherds:

> "And he [Jacob] blessed Joseph, saying: The God in whose ways my fathers Abraham and Isaac walked, **the God who has been my shepherd** from my birth to this day...bless the lads [Ephraim and Manasseh]. In them may my name be recalled, and the names of my fathers..." (Genesis 48:15-16)

The idyllic picture of God as the shepherd existed even centuries later when the majority of Israelites were no longer shepherds themselves:

> "Like a shepherd He pastures His flock: He gathers the lambs in His arms and carries them in His bosom; gently He drives the ewes." (Isaiah 40:11)

> "On the day of salvation...they shall pasture along the roads, on every bare height shall be their

Then the wolf harries the flock and scatters the sheep...I am the good shepherd. As the Father knows me and I know the Father, in the same way I know my sheep and they know me. And I am willing to die for them."
(John 10:11-15)

"A lion got into a shepherd's flock and ravaged and devoured them. Whom does one comfort if not the owner of the flock! So the Blessed One says: My people were lost sheep; their shepherds led them astray. (Jeremiah 50:6)"
(Midrash Zota Ekha [Lamentations] 1,12)

upper right: *Who knows what danger lurks behind the bend?*

37

"Whom did Moses resemble? A faithful shepherd: when the fence broke down close to darkness, he repaired it on three sides. One side remained broken but he did not have the needed hour of daylight to fix it, so he blocked the break with his own body. A lion came and he chased it off; a wolf came and he chased it off...." (Ruth Rabbah, Preface, 5)

18. Moses and the thirsty kid
"Our Sages said that when Moses was tending the flock of Jethro in the desert, a little kid escaped from him. He ran after it until it reached a shady place. When it reached the shady place, a pool of water became visible and the kid stopped to drink. When Moses approached it, he said: I did not know you ran away because of thirst; you must be weary. So he placed the kid on his shoulders and walked back. Thereupon God said: Because you had mercy in tending the flock of a man, you will certainly tend My flock, Israel. Hence, 'Now Moses was tending the flock...' (Exodus 3:1)" (Shmot Rabbah 2, 2)

pasture; they shall not hunger or thirst; hot wind and sun shall not strike them; for He who loves them will lead them, He will guide them to springs of water." (Isaiah 49:8, 9-10)

More than any other prophet, Jeremiah is steeped in the landscapes of the desert and the life of shepherds and sheep. And consequently, more than all the other prophets, Jeremiah deals with the failure of the nation's leaders to fulfill the task of the shepherd vis-à-vis both the "sheep" and the "Supreme Owner of the flock."

"The priests no longer asked, 'Where is the Lord?' The guardians of the law ignored Me, **the shepherds of the people rebelled against Me**; the prophets prophesied in the name of Baal, and followed gods powerless to help." (Jeremiah 2:8)

"Oh **shepherds who let the flock of My pasture stray and scatter!**...Thus said the Lord, the God of Israel, concerning the shepherds who should tend My people: It is you who let My flock scatter and go astray. You did not count them, but I am going to have you account for your wicked acts...And I Myself will gather the remnant of My flock from all the lands to which I have banished them, and I will bring them back to their pasture, where they shall be fertile and increase. And **I will appoint over them shepherds who will tend them; they shall no longer fear** or be dismayed, and none of them shall be missing." (Jeremiah 23:1- 4)

"**For the shepherds were mere brutes** and did not seek the Lord; therefore they were not aware and all their flock is scattered." (Jeremiah 10:21)

"My people were lost sheep: **their shepherds misled them**, the hills led them astray; they roamed from mount to hill, they forgot their own resting place." (Jeremiah 50:6)

The prophet Zechariah sounds the same note:

> "That is why My people have strayed like a flock, **they suffer for lack of a shepherd. My anger is roused against the shepherds**, and I will [also] punish the rams. For the Lord of Hosts will count His flock, the House of Judah..."
>
> (Zechariah 10:2-3)

> "Thus said my God the Lord: Tend the sheep meant for slaughter, whose owners will slaughter them with impunity...and **whose shepherd will not pity them.**" (Zechariah 11:4-5)

Interesting, and quite astonishing at first glance, is the fact that one of the most impressive Biblical descriptions of shepherding and its comparison to the responsibilities of the nation's leaders is given by the prophet Ezekiel, who was not a shepherd at all, but a priest in Jerusalem who must have served in the Temple :

"Prophesy, man, about the shepherds of Israel. Prophesy, and say to them: You shepherds of Israel who care only for themselves, these are the words of the Lord God: Should not the shepherd care for the sheep? You consume the milk, wear the wool, and slaughter the fatlings, but you do not feed the sheep. You have not encouraged the weary, tended the sick, bandaged the hurt, recovered the straggler, or searched for the lost; and even the strong you have driven with ruthless severity. They are scattered, they have no shepherd, they may become the prey of wild beasts. My sheep go straying over the mountains and on every high hill. My flock is dispersed over the face of the earth, with no one to ask after them or search for them. Therefore, you shepherds, hear the words of the Lord. As surely as I live, says the Lord God, because My sheep are ravaged by wild beasts and have become their prey for lack of a shepherd, because My shepherds have not asked after the sheep but have cared only for themselves and not for the sheep — therefore, you shepherds, hear the words of the Lord God: I am going to deal with the shepherds. I will demand a reckoning of them for My flock; and I will dismiss them from tending the flock. The shepherds shall care only for themselves no longer, for I will rescue My flock from their jaws, and they shall feed on them no more.

"For these are the words of the Lord God: Now I myself will ask after My sheep and go in search of them. As a shepherd goes in search of his sheep when some in his flock have become separated, so I will search out My sheep and rescue them, no matter where they were scattered on dark and cloudy days. I will bring them out from every nation, gather them in from other lands, and lead them home to their own soil. I will graze them on the mountains of Israel, by her streams and in all her green fields. I will feed them on good grazing land and their pasture shall be the high mountains of Israel. There they will rest, there in good pasture, and find rich grazing on the mountains of Israel. I Myself will tend My flock, I Myself will pen them in their fold, says the Lord God. I will search for the lost, recover the straggler, bandage the hurt, strengthen the sick; and the fat and the bullying ones I will destroy. I will tend them as they deserve. (19)

"As for you, my flock, these are the words of the Lord God: I will judge between one sheep and another. You rams and bucks! Is it not enough for you to graze on choice grazing land, but you must also trample with your feet what is left from your grazing? And is it not enough for you to drink clear water but you must also muddy the rest with your feet? And must My flock graze on what your feet have trampled and drink what your feet have muddied? These, therefore, are the words of the Lord God to them: Here am I. I am going to decide between the fat animals and the lean, because you pushed with flank and shoulder against the feeble ones and butted them with your horns until you scattered them abroad. I will save My flock and they shall no longer be ravaged. I will judge between one sheep and another.

"Then I will appoint a single shepherd over them to tend them — My servant David. He shall tend them and he shall be a shepherd to them."   (Ezekiel 34:2-24)

As opposed to Jeremiah, who lived the life of a shepherd and reflected this experience in most of his prophecies, Ezekiel was a member of urban "high society," part of Jerusalem's

19. Separating the sheep from the goats
Although sheep and goats both belong to the category of small cattle called *tzon* צאן in Hebrew, there is a marked difference in the grazing habits of each species. Sheep crop at an even height several centimeters above ground level. The goat, on the other hand, not only crops much closer to the ground, but also tears leaves, buds, and fruit off trees. The goat's unsavory reputation is clearly expressed in the New Testament words concerning the Day of Judgment: "When the Son of Man comes...he will separate men into two groups, **as a shepherd separates the sheep from the goats,** and he will place the sheep on his right hand and the goats on his left...Then he will say to those on his left hand: The curse is upon you; go from my sight to the eternal fire...And they will go away to eternal punishment, but the righteous will enter eternal life." (Matthew 25:31-33, 41, 46)

41

20. Ezekiel and the Dead Sea

Two prophets saw visions foretelling the day when fresh water would flow from Jerusalem to the Dead Sea. Zechariah saw a vision in which the Mount of Olives split in half, reminding his audience of "the earthquake in the days of King Uzziah of Judah" (Zechariah 14:5). "In that day, fresh water shall flow from Jerusalem, part of it to the Eastern Sea [Dead Sea] and part to the Far Sea [Mediterranean Sea], throughout the summer and winter." (Zechariah 14:8)

Ezekiel, as expected from his pedantic nature, describes his vision in vivid and realistic detail:

"He led me back to the entrance of the Temple, and I found that water was issuing from below the platform of the Temple...As the man went eastward with a measuring line in his hand, he measured off a thousand cubits and led me across the water; the water was ankle deep. Then he measured off another thousand and led me across the water; the water was knee deep. He measured off a further thousand and led me across the water; the water was up to the waist. When he measured yet another thousand, it was a stream I could not cross; for the water had swollen into a stream that could not be crossed except by swimming. 'Do you see, O mortal?' he said to me; and he led me back to the bank of the stream.

"When I returned to the bank, I saw trees in great profusion on both banks of the stream. 'This water,' he told me, 'runs out to the eastern region and flows into the *Arava*; and when it comes into the sea, into the sea of foul waters [Dead Sea], the water will be healed. Every living creature that swarms will be able to live wherever this stream goes; the fish will be abundant once these waters have reached there. It will be healed and

nobility exiled by Nebuchadnezzar to Babylon together with Jehoiakhin, king of Jerusalem, in 597 BCE. Doubtless Ezekiel was acquainted with the nation's leaders, their customs and life-style. Before the exile he was a member of the priestly family in Jerusalem, so it is not surprising that he was familiar with the Temple ritual. (Beginning in chapter 40 Ezekiel even blueprints the future rebuilt Holy Temple.) But how did he come to know "professional" shepherding in such extraordinary detail?

In fact, aside from this one chapter, which is amazing in its minute descriptions of the habits of sheep and the tasks of the shepherd, there is nothing in Ezekiel's style that reflects an affinity for the shepherd's life or a spiritual closeness to the landscapes of the desert's grazing regions. It is reasonable to assume that he became informed about the work of the shepherd through his acquaintance with the chief herdsmen who brought to the priests the animals for sacrifice. Possibly Ezekiel joined the chief herdsmen in their sojourns in the Judean Desert, the Valley of Jericho, and the Dead Sea area[20] and so became familiar with the life of the shepherd and his responsibility for the flocks. This is why his anger was kindled against those leaders whom he knew at close range, whose treatment of the common people so blatantly contrasted with the shepherd's treatment of his flock. Furthermore,

Chunks of salt floating on the Dead Sea **opposite page:** *Salt marshes at the southern end of the Dead Sea*

Ezekiel's words ring with scathing censure of the members of that same "high society" who butt forward, not caring that they trample the weak in the process: "you pushed with flank and shoulder against the feeble ones and butted them with your horns until you scattered them abroad..."

We return at this juncture to the same short verse with which the chapter began:

"The Lord is my shepherd, I shall not want."

(Psalm 23:1)

These few words echo the vision of the prophets who saw in the Lord God of Israel the ideal shepherd who cares for all His flocks' needs, and in whose image the prophets wanted to see the nation's leaders.

But this chapter is not complete without the following:

"The Lord is my shepherd, I shall not want..., said Rabbi Yose bar Hanina[21]: **You will find that there is no more scorned profession in the world than that of the shepherd,** who all his life walks with his staff and his knapsack, **yet David calls the Blessed One, Shepherd! David said: Because Jacob called Him Shepherd...I too shall call Him Shepherd: The Lord is my shepherd, I shall not want.**" (Midrash [22] Tehilim, Psalm 23)

"...speaking of David, King of Israel [23] when he was tending his father's flocks, and suddenly was made king...all said: **Till now he was a shepherd and suddenly he is king?** And he answered: You wonder about me! I wonder

everything will live wherever this stream goes. Fishermen shall stand beside it all the way from Ein-Gedi to Ein Eglaim; it shall be a place for drying nets; and the fish will be of various kinds and most plentiful, like the fish of the Great [Mediterranean] Sea. But its marshes and rock hollow pools shall not be healed; they shall be left as saltpans. All kinds of trees for food will grow on both banks of the stream. Their leaves will not wither nor their fruit fail; they will yield new fruit every month, because the water for them flows from the Temple. Their fruit will serve for food and their leaves for medication.'" (Ezekiel 47:1-12)

The obvious distinction made by Ezekiel between the waters of the Dead Sea that shall be "healed" and teeming with life and the marshes and pools that shall "not be healed" so that they may continue to be the source of salt, indicates that Ezekiel was well acquainted with the Dead Sea.

This is what Joseph Braslavi writes in his comprehensive study, *Round and Round the Dead Sea*, (Hakibbutz Hameuhad, Tel Aviv, 1956, pp. 32-33):

"Clear indicators of high and low water marks [in the Dead Sea] are the rock hollow pools, puddles, sediments and hard salt crusts along the shoreline: in a period of high water the sea covers strip after strip of land, and when the water recedes, it leaves behind pools of standing water. The water left in the rock hollow pools, in fissures, and in the marshes evaporates, leaving behind the salt it had contained. In the days of Turkish rule [in the late 19th-early 20th century], the Bedouin collected this salt and sold it in the marketplaces of Israel. Today they no longer do that. This phenomenon can be useful in explaining the prophecy of Ezekiel 47:10-11, where he says: 'Fishermen shall stand beside it all the way from Ein-Gedi to Ein Eglaim; it shall be a place for drying nets; and the fish will be of various kinds and most plentiful, like the fish of the Great Sea. But its marshes and rock hollow pools shall not be healed; they shall be left as saltpans.' In other words, the waters of the Dead Sea will become sweet and filled with fish, but the marshes and rock hollow pools which surround the Dead Sea at the high water mark will not. In future, these will continue to supply salt."

Ezekiel's familiarity with the Dead Sea is obvious also from the following: "On that day I will assign to Gog a burial site there in Israel. It shall be in the valley that blocks the path of travelers who try to pass east of the [Dead] sea. There Gog and all his multitude will be buried. It shall be called the Valley of Gog's Multitude. The House of Israel shall...bury them, in order to cleanse the land...And they shall appoint men to serve permanently, to traverse the land and bury any [bodies] that remain above ground, in order to cleanse it...As those who traverse the country make their rounds, any one of them who sees a human bone shall erect a marker beside it, until the buriers have interred them in the Valley of Gog's Multitude." (Ezekiel 39:11-15) In order to cleanse and purify the land of the corpses left after the defeat of Gog, Ezekiel envisions the burial of the dead far to the east of the Dead Sea where the mudflats are in any event a natural barrier to travelers.

21. Rabbi Yose bar Hanina — second generation *amora* in Israel (250-290 CE); important member of the Academy of Tiberias.

22. midrash מדרש — the designation of a particular genre of rabbinic literature

about myself even more than you! It was the Holy Spirit that answered them: **It was from God.**"
(Midrash Tehilim, Psalm 118:21)

Chief herdsman — head of the Sanhedrin

These homilies, written at least 1,300 years after David grazed his father's flocks in the desert, testify to the **ambivalent feelings about the shepherd that evolved with passing generations**. After the destruction of the Second Temple and the terrible wars that devastated Israel in the ensuing years, unavoidable conflict arose between the shepherds who took advantage of the increase in thickets and forests and the landowners who wanted to reclaim their fields for cultivation. (The conflict consequently led to the strict injunctions limiting grazing mentioned earlier.) At the same time, because the Bible was the undisputed font of all of the Oral Law (the Talmud — Mishnah and Gemara), there was a deep desire to preserve and even strengthen the ancient traditions that honored the shepherd and his abilities and raised him to the highest status.

On the one hand we have a sense of general suspicion towards the shepherd, considered a robber, barred from bearing witness:

"Said Rav Yehuda [24]: An ordinary shepherd is disqualified [from giving testimony]. (Baba Metzia 5b) Rashi's commentary explains: **"A shepherd, even when there is no witness against him [that he grazes in other people's fields], is disqualified from giving testimony, because the assumption is that he is a robber, since he is always suspect of grazing in fields belonging to others."**

"Rabbi Yishmael said: My father's family belonged to the property owners in Upper Galilee. **Why were they ruined?** Because they allowed their flocks to graze in the thickets...**And even though the thickets were very near their property, there was also a small field** [belonging to others] **nearby, and they** [my father's family] **allowed their flocks to pass through it.**" [25] (Baba Kama 80a)

And yet there is a great deal of understanding and forgiveness in the following:

"Just as sheep, even when they damage trees, are not held

constituting an anthology of homilies, presenting both Biblical exegesis and sermons, and forming a running commentary on specific books of the Bible.

23. The poor man's lamb

Nathan, the prophet who admonished King David for his sin with Bathsheba, wife of Uriah the Hittite, used a very personal parable to catch David's undivided attention.

"There were two men in the same city, one rich and one poor, the rich man had very large flocks and herds, but the poor man had only one little ewe lamb that he had bought. He tended it and it grew up together with him and his children: it used to share his morsel of bread, drink from his cup, and nestle in his bosom; it was like a daughter to him. One day, a traveler came to the rich man, but he was loath to take anything from his own flocks or herds to prepare a meal for the guest who had come to him, so he took the poor man's lamb and prepared it for the man who had come to him."(II Samuel 12:1-4)

Quite intentionally Nathan chose the parable of the poor man's lamb: Nathan had to ensure an immediate royal judgment that would leave David no room for consideration or doubt. Therefore Nathan chose a parable that would instantly capture David's attention and emotions, linked as it was to his days as a shepherd, when he certainly must have experienced a special affection for a lamb or ewe that attached itself to him and may have been with him in his tent or cave. And, indeed, David passes sentence even before Nathan finishes the parable: "David flew into a rage against the man, and said to Nathan: As the Lord lives, the man who did this deserves to die!" (II Samuel 12:5)

24. Rav Yehuda (bar Yehezkel) one of the greatest Babylonian *amoraim* of the second generation (250-290 CE); founder of the Academy of Pumbedita.

25. Tethered to the bedpost
The Gemara relates an incident that vividly illustrates how meticulous the Sages were in following the ruling concerning the raising of sheep and goats only in the desert and thickets: "His disciples asked Rabban Gamliel [*] whether it is permissible to breed sheep or goats. He replied: It is permitted. But did we not learn: It is forbidden [outside the specified regions]. What they actually asked was this: May it be kept around temporarily for an immediate need? He said to them: It is permissible, provided it does not go out to pasture with the flock, but is fastened to the bedpost. Our rabbis taught: There was once a certain pious person who suffered from heart trouble, and the physicians said the only hope for his recovery was for him to suck warm milk every morning. A goat was therefore brought to him and fastened to the legs of the bed, and he sucked from it every morning. After some days his colleagues came to visit him, but as soon as they noticed the goat fastened to the legs of the bed they turned back and said: An armed robber is in the house of this man, how can we come in to see him? They thereupon sat down and inquired into his conduct, but they did not find any fault in him except this sin of the goat. He also at the time of his death proclaimed: I know that no sin can be imputed to me save that of the goat, when I transgressed against the words of my colleagues."
(Baba Kama 80b)

[*] Rabban Gamliel (of Yavne) second generation of *tannaim* (80-110 CE); for about 30 years after the destruction of the Second Temple, he was the president *(nasi)* of the Sanhedrin

responsible by their owners, so also even though Israel sins, God treats them like a flock." (Midrash Shmot Rabbah 24, 3)

However, when it came to the daily problems, the precepts of this last midrash were not followed; the assumption was that the shepherd is suspect not only of robbery but even of literally stealing from the owner, and this was the way the rabbinic ruling was formulated:

"It is not permitted to buy from shepherds either milk or fleece...The principle is that anything the absence of which, if it is sold by the shepherd, would be noticed by the owner [of the flock] may be bought from the shepherd, but if the owner would not notice it, it may not be bought [from the shepherd]." (Baba Kama 118b)

In certain periods, this negative attitude to grazing and shepherds reached such extremes that **a shepherd who decided to change his occupation was considered a "repentant"** and on this basis was permitted to sell his flock gradually so that he would not suffer undue financial hardship.

"Said the Sages: A shepherd who repented is not required to sell [all his flock] immediately, but he may sell it by degrees." (Baba Kama 80a)

On the other hand, we see from the Sages a continuation of the tradition of great respect for the shepherd's special competence; so much so that the title **"chief herdsman"** alluded in their day to **the president of the court of justice and the head of the Sanhedrin**:

"Doeg the Edomite was **the president of the court**, because '[he was] Saul's chief herdsman.' (I Samuel 21:8)." (Midrash Tehilim, Psalm 3:4)

"Let us learn from Doeg who was **the head of the Sanhedrin**, because: '[he was] Saul's chief herdsman.' (I Samuel 21:8)." (Midrash Tehilim, Psalm 52:3)

"Said Rav: [26] Ezekiel complained to God: Lord of the Universe, am I not a priest and a prophet? Why did Isaiah prophesy in Jerusalem while I prophesy in exile?...And should you say that they [the other prophets in Jerusalem] prophesied good and I evil? No! For I prophesied good and they evil! Imagine, for instance, to what this can be compared: To a flesh and blood king who had many servants whom he appointed over his kingdom. **The wisest among them he made the shepherd.** The wise one began to protest and said: My companions are in the settlement and I am in the desert? So Ezekiel says: All my companions are in Jerusalem and I am in exile?" (Midrash, The Vision of Ezekiel 80b)

In summary, we have seen that the image of the shepherd in Jewish tradition was shaped by two intertwined factors: the history of the people of Israel and the unique geography of Israel. A nation of shepherds, which carried with it memories of the landscapes of the Sinai Desert and the events during their wandering in it, settled in a hilly land of rainy zones covered with evergreen forests adjacent to arid regions capable of yielding only grazing vegetation. The nation of shepherds transformed the forested hills into terraced agricultural land and switched to farming. However, shepherding did not cease. Rather the pasture of sheep and goats was limited to areas that the farmers could not utilize.

The prophets saw the days of the nation's nomadic wandering in the Sinai Desert as the period of young love, when the belief in one God was the unshakeable faith of all the people. For this reason those bygone days appeared to the prophets as a period to which the nation had to return temporarily in order to cleanse itself of the worship of idols with which it was afflicted as a consequence of the shift to agricultural life. An ideal image evolved of the leader as shepherd, capable of leading the flock through all the dangers in the harsh extremes of the desert. This image permeated the Biblically rooted homilies of the Sages. On the other hand, rabbinic rulings, responding to changing needs and conditions, reflected a more practical approach to the shepherd and the consequences of his activity, which could, in certain situations, be destructive. [27]

which was then located in Yavne. He was not only the chief religious authority of his time, but also the accepted national-political leader, recognized by the Roman government as spokesman for the Jews.

26. Rav (Abba bar Aivo or Abba Arikha, "the Tall") — the first of the Babylonian *amoraim* (220-250 CE); founded the Academy of Sura.

27. It pays to dream of goats
Contrary to the incident of the goat that was dubbed "an armed robber" even though it was tied to the bedpost of a critically ill man, and was counted as a sin against him on his deathbed, it is amusing to read the following in the Talmudic Tractate Berakhot (Blessings): "Said Rabbi Yosef [*]: He who dreams of a goat, his year will be blessed; if he dreams about goats, his years shall be blessed, as it is written: The goats' milk will suffice for your food. (Proverbs 27:27)" (Berakhot 57a)

But it is important to note the differences in time and place between these two stories: the incident of the goat tied to the bedpost took place in Israel during the time of Rabban Gamliel of Yavne, just a few years after the destruction of the Second Temple, when enormous efforts were being made to restore the destroyed agricultural base. Understandably, the farmer considered goats a major enemy — one of the most voracious despoilers of cultivated land. On the other hand, Rav Yosef taught in Babylon some 200 years later. His only concern was to comment on the Biblical verse — he had no reason to infer anything relating to daily livelihood problems in the Land of Israel.

[*]**Rabbi Yosef (bar Hiyya)** — third generation *amora* (290-320 CE); head of the Pumbedita Academy in Babylon.

Chapter II

"He maketh me to lie down in green pastures;
He leadeth me beside the still waters." (Psalm 23:2)

Green pastures in the desert

"The pastures in the desert are rich with blessing and the hills are girded with joy."   (Psalm 65:13)

We have seen that for many centuries grazing continued in Israel side by side with farming, albeit limited to uncultivated areas that were generally called *midbar* in the Bible, consistently translated here as **desert**.[1] Among these areas were also thickets and forests where perennial wild vegetation flourished, the ideal fodder for sheep and goats. We also discussed the green pastureland in the Jordan Valley and mentioned the wide expanses of grazing area that existed in the days of Lot; during a period of extraordinarily low water level these green areas covered the mouths of the wadis that flow into the Dead Sea. But **where and when did the shepherds pasture their flocks in those desert areas between the mountains and the *Arava* — the Rift Valley** (those areas that are leeward of the moisture-bearing winds) called by many Biblical names, including: Midbar Ziph and Midbar Maon, Midbar Tekoa, Midbar Yehuda, and Midbar Ein Gedi?

The conditions change in these deserts from year to year, from month to month, and sometimes even from week to week. In rainy years there are some regions in the northern Judean Desert on which 400 mm (16 inches) or more of rain may fall. In such an especially rainy winter these areas are covered by a carpet of greenery interspersed with a myriad of red, purple, and yellow flowers. These carpets are a refreshing sight, delighting both shepherd and flock. Such a year is described in the sixty-fifth psalm, entitled "For the leader: A psalm of David. A song:"

> "You crown the year with Your bounty, plenty flourishes in Your paths; the pasturelands flourish, the hills are girded with joy. The meadows are clothed with flocks, the valleys mantled with grain; they raise a shout, they break into song."   (Psalm 65:12-14)

The flowering of the desert in such a year serves Isaiah in his prophecy concerning the longed-for return of the Children of Israel from exile:

1. Which are "desert" animals and which "household" animals? To define which flocks are considered "household" (i.e., domestic) and which "desert" or grazing ones, different methods were used in selecting the suitable seasons for grazing, evidently varying by region and by the rainfall of a particular year:

"Desert animals are such as are led out about Passover [March-April] and graze in [more distant] pasture lands, and who are led back in at the time of the first rainfall [in a normal year, October-November]. Household animals are such as are led out and graze outside the settlement but return and spend each night inside the settlement. Rabbi [*] says: Both of these are household animals; but desert animals are such as are led out and graze in [more distant] pasture lands and who do not return to the habitation of men either in summer or in winter." (Beitza 40a)

[*] **Rabbi (Yehuda HaNasi)** — the redactor of the Mishnah; leading light of the sixth and last generation of *tannaim* (170-200 CE).

49

"The arid desert shall be glad, the wilderness shall rejoice and shall blossom like a tulip. It shall blossom abundantly, it shall also exult and sing. It shall receive the glory of Lebanon, the splendor of Carmel and Sharon..."   (Isaiah 35:1-2)

But there are years in which rainfall in the desert barely suffices for a sparse green carpet to cover only the northern and western slopes of the desert hills, and this for but a few short weeks. Sometimes the winter precipitation is so scant that there is no green cover whatsoever on the hills, and the only patches of vegetation are found in the beds of the wadis. Under normal conditions, perennial desert shrubs produce new leaves and shoots with the coming of the rain. But in periods of drought they are able to survive, as they do in summer, without any leaves or with only the most vestigial leaf cover undiscernible to the untrained eye. A description of such a drought year is found in chapter 14 of the book of Jeremiah, where he describes, among the catastrophic results:

> "Even the doe in the field forsook her newborn fawn because there was no grass. And the wild horses stood on the bare heights snuffing the air like owls; their eyes failed because there is no food."
>
> (Jeremiah 14:5-6)

The above-mentioned phenomena lead me to believe that the words from the twenty-third psalm, **"He maketh me to lie down in green pastures,"** express much more than the simple fact that a shepherd knows to bring his flocks to good grazing land. Because the psalm speaks of God, the Shepherd, (whether of the individual — the psalmist — or of the entire nation) it is a cry of thanksgiving that **He Himself sends the rains at a time and in a quantity that ensure green pastures as a resting place**.

Usually, when the sheep and goats reach green pastures they are in constant motion, grazing and foraging. **The repose described here in the green pastures paints a picture of ultimate satiation after abundant feeding**.

A gathering place in the desert and the Holy of Holies in the Temple

> "...I will bring together the remnant of Israel; I will make them all like sheep of Bozrah [2], like a **flock in its meadow** (*dovro* דברו)— they will be noisy with people."
>
> (Micah 2:12)

> "Then lambs shall graze **as in their meadows** (*dovram* דוברם)..."
>
> (Isaiah 5:17)

The word *dovro* דברו evidently refers to **a central place to which the flock is brought or where it gathers**. It contains the three root letters, *dalet, bet, reish* ד-ב-ר, which are the root for the word *midbar* מדבר, usually translated as desert. Those letters also form an Aramaic word related to

2. The best grazing land
Bozrah was a town generally believed to be the same as "Betzer in the desert, in the plains" (Joshua 20:8) in the territory of the tribe of Reuben, east of the Jordan River. The people of the tribe of Reuben were shepherds who asked Moses for the land best suited for grazing.

3. Why was the name of the town changed from Kiryat Sefer to Dvir?

"In accordance with the Lord's command to Joshua, Caleb...was given a portion among the tribe of Judah, namely, Kiryat Arba...that is, Hebron. Caleb dislodged from there the three Anakites...From there he marched against the inhabitants of Dvir [Debir] – the name of Dvir was formerly Kiryat Sefer – and Caleb announced, 'I will give my daughter Akhsah in marriage to the man who attacks and captures Kiryat Sefer. His kinsman Othniel...captured it, and Caleb gave him his daughter Akhsah in marriage. When she came [to Othniel], she induced him to ask her father for some property... 'Give me a present; for you have given me [dry] Negev land, so give me springs of water.' And he gave her [the springs of] upper and lower Gulloth." (Joshua 15:13-17, 19)

Dvir (which the Biblical archaeologist William Albright identified as Tel-Bet-Marsim, some 20 km northeast of Beersheva and about 25 km southwest of Hebron) lies on the edge of the Negev Desert. There is extensive pastureland in the hills south of the settlement. I believe the name Dvir indicates that the place was a fold for the flocks (*mirbatz ha-adarim* מרבץ העדרים), a kind of "regional capital" for the Negev shepherds. This would explain the name change before its capture by Othniel from Kiryat Sefer (according to the *Archaeological Encyclopaedia of Israel*, the name means "the auditor's granaries") to Dvir. The name was changed because of the functional change from a regional storehouse for grain in the Canaanite period when the areas to the north and west were farmed, to a regional goat and sheepfold *(dvir* דביר*)* center where

midbar, davar [דבר] meaning **a place to which the flocks are driven or led**.[3]

The word with the same root letters, *dvir* דביר, is the name for the **Holy of Holies** in the Temple in Jerusalem. Therefore it seems to me that this name for the Holy of Holies is also connected to the concept of the *dover* דבר in the desert in **the symbolic sense of a place of repose in green pastures, where the flocks safely gather and rest.**[4]

The same line of reasoning enriches understanding of another phrase in Jeremiah:

"My people were lost sheep; their shepherds misled them. The hills led them astray; they roamed from mount to hill, they forgot their own resting place. All who encountered them devoured them; and their foes said: We shall not be held guilty, because they have sinned against **the Lord, the just Pasture** (*neve tzedek* נוה צדק), **the Hope of their father** (*mikve avotehem* מקוה אבותיהם) – the Lord." (Jeremiah 50:6-7)

Jeremiah uses a special phrase here to describe an attribute of God: *mikve avotehem* מקוה אבותיהם, usually translated, as in the Jewish Publication Society's translation above, as "the hope of their fathers," as if the word comes from the Hebrew root **k-v-h** קוה, to hope. But from the same root another

Goats gather towards evening in their pen

Hebrew verb is derived, meaning to **gather**: "Let the waters below the sky be **gathered together** into one place." (Genesis 1:9) This meaning of the same root leads us to understand this phrase, *mikve avotehem* מקוה אבותיהם, as the **gathering place where the sheep rest**, and not from *tikva* תקוה meaning hope.[5] This supposition is consistent with Jeremiah's expression **"true"** or **"just Pasture"** (*neve tzedek* נוה צדק), which parallels his **"pasture for shepherds"** (*neve ro'im* נוה רועים) where they can rest their flocks. (Jeremiah 33:12)

The phrase **"just Pasture"** (*neve tzedek* נוה צדק), used as an attribute of God by Jeremiah, is also used by him in connection with the **Temple Mount:**

> "Thus said the Lord of Hosts, the God of Israel: They shall again say this in the land of Judah and in its towns, when I restore their fortunes: [May] the Lord [Who is the] **just Pasture** [and] the **holy mountain,** bless you!" (Jeremiah 31:22)

The sense of sheep pens in the grazing areas being **places of repose and ingathering** is also felt in other of Jeremiah's verses **if we translate** *mikve israel* מקוה ישראל not in the conventional way of **"Hope of Israel"** but as **"Gathering Point of Israel:"**

Goat and sheep pens in the Judean Desert stand empty at the end of summer as shepherds take the flocks for grazing to the plain of the Jordan.

shepherds and their flocks gathered. The shepherds were all members of the same families belonging to the tribe of Judah who continued the shepherding tradition in this area.

The same logic holds true even if Dvir is identified as Hirbet Ravud (as it is by Moshe Kukhbi, *Guide to Israel*, volume on Judea, p. 187), which is also located in the borderline desert area between farmland and the Negev hills, close to the crossroads of Hebron-Beersheva and the turnoff to the village of Samoa.

4. Commentators and dictionaries on *dvir* דביר

Rashi in his commentary on I Kings 6:5: "The Holy of the Holies is the *dvir* דביר." Metzudat Zion writes of the same verse: "The Holy of the Holies was called *dvir* דביר because the Word (*dibur* דבור) came forth from there." In Ben-Yehuda's [*] dictionary: "In each building, the rear part, especially in the Temple in Jerusalem where the section to the rear of the building was holiest, the place where the Ark was placed."

[*] **Eliezer Ben-Yehuda** – (1858-1922) the "father" of modern Hebrew.

5. "The length of crimson cord"

The Bible relates a story of the Jericho harlot Rahab who aided Joshua's spies and as a reward was granted her one request that her family be saved from destruction when the Israelites captured the city. The spies instructed her to mark her house on the city wall by lowering a "length of crimson cord" from her window. (Joshua 2:18, 21) The original Hebrew uses the word *tikva* תקוה, which obviously cannot mean "hope" in this context. Yet could a "length of cord," of whatever thickness, and of even the brightest red, have been visible in the dust as the walls of Jericho crumbled and the Israelites poured into the city? Hardly. Therefore the word *tikva* תקוה means here a "gathering together" of thread, in other words, an object on which the thread is wound – in short, a **skein**. A ball or skein of bright crimson would have been much more noticeable! (In fact, Yehuda Keal, in his commentary on the book of Joshua [*Da'at Mikra*, Rav Kook Press, Jerusalem, 1983], mentions the possibility of such an interpretation.)

"O **Gathering Point** of Israel, its Deliverer in time of trouble..."   (Jeremiah 14:8)

"O **Gathering Point** of Israel! O Lord! All who forsake You shall be put to shame...for they have forsaken the Lord, the Fount of living waters."
                                                    (Jeremiah 17:13)

I believe that even the next verse becomes much clearer in the general context of the events described in I Chronicles 28 and 29 if *mikve* is understood as a "gathering place" and not hope.

"For we are sojourners with You, mere transients like our fathers; our days on earth are like a shadow and there is no gathering place *[mikve]*."
                                                    (I Chronicles 29:15)

The phrase "our days on earth are like a shadow" is usually understood to signify the shortness of the human life-span, and the next phrase, "and there is no *mikve*," is usually translated as "with no abiding" or "nothing in prospect," in other words, with no hope of extending one's life. But if *mikve* is understood to refer to a gathering place, where the flock is united, it ties together much more logically in the context of the story in I Chronicles, which quotes part of a speech given by David "in front of all the assemblage" (I Chronicles 29:10) just before "they again proclaimed Solomon son of David king." (I Chronicles 29:22) The description begins in the previous chapter and reiterates the task that David bequeaths to Solomon: the building of the Holy Temple in Jerusalem as the permanent focus of the nation. Therefore, it seems to me that the words "we were **strangers** with You, **mere transients like our fathers**" express the idea that so long as this permanent center is not built, there is something transient and nomadic in the Israelite settlement of the Land of Israel, as was true in earlier generations ("like our fathers"). This notion also fits the expression **"our days on earth are like a shadow,"** which underscores the idea of constant passage (like the fleeting shadow) from one temporary site to another. The words **"there is no abiding place"** complete the picture and emphasize that there is yet **no nucleus that can gather the nation.** David assigns the building of this focal point to Solomon as his first task upon assuming the monarchy.

In conclusion, it is possible to understand that the Holy of Holies (*dvir* דביר) in the Temple in Jerusalem was a symbol of the place where the flock was penned. The flock, of course, was the nation of Israel, and the Holy of Holies was that focal point to which the Shepherd drives His flock and where all the nation's hopes and prayers gather.

Water in the desert: treacherous waters and still waters

"Water revives one in the desert; honey does not."
(Tosefta Baba Kama 10, 28)

"Two men are in the desert. One has a jug of water and the other a jug of honey. The rabbinic court ruled that if the water jug cracks, the one with the jug of honey spills out the honey and saves his companion's water. When they reach a settlement, the first one pays his companion for his honey, because water is vital in the desert and honey is not."
(Tosefta Baba Kama 10, 28)

There is no more faithful testimony than this rabbinic ruling that life in the desert was an integral part of Israel's cultural makeup even after most of the nation had not lived in the desert for many generations. This ruling demonstrates awareness of the paramount danger of dehydration in the desert. Today, the strict rule for any excursion into Israel's deserts, whether for pleasure or army maneuvers, calls for providing water for all needs. But it is not always possible to carry sufficient water, especially if the sojourn in the desert is extended. In such cases it is vital to plan the route along known and certain sources of water, because the availability of water is the most important factor in desert survival.

The problem of the lack of water in the desert is emphasized by the first stories dealing with the wandering of the Children of Israel in the desert, immediately following the crossing of the Red [Reed] Sea:

6. Bitter "heals" bitter

The Sages asked what was the tree that sweetened the bitter waters of Marah. "...Rabbi Yehoshua ben Korha (*) said it is oleander wood...Rabban Shimon ben Gamliel said: See how different are the ways of God from those of mortal men: mortal man heals bitterness with sweetening, but the Lord...heals bitterness with bitterness. How? He put that which causes injury into the injured thing and so makes a miracle..." (Yalkut Shimoni 1, 256 and in other sources). Clearly, in their search for the tree that Moses used, the Sages were not looking for a plant that could really sweeten bitter water. They asked themselves which plant was used **for the miracle**. Rabbi Yehoshua ben Korha's suggestion was probably based

"They walked three days in the desert and found no water. They came to Marah, but they could not drink the water of Marah because it was bitter; that is why it was named Marah [Bitter]. And the people grumbled against Moses, saying: What shall we drink? So he cried out to the Lord, and the Lord showed him a tree; he threw it into the water and the water became sweet...[6] And they came to Elim, where there were twelve springs of water and seventy palm trees; and they encamped there beside the water." (Exodus 15:22-27)

Only after the Bible relates the resolution of the water problem does it go on to tell of the daily allotment of manna from heaven for food. The lack of water and the raging thirst during the wandering in the Sinai Desert were an intrinsic part of the experience of that desert generation and remained deeply etched in the nation's collective memory:

"Take care lest you forget the Lord your God...and your heart grow haughty and you forget the Lord your God who freed you from the land of Egypt, the house of bondage; who led you through **the great and terrible desert** of...serpents and scorpions, **and thirst with no water in it...**" (Deuteronomy 8:11-15)

Some 500 years after the period of the wandering in the desert, the national consciousness and memory were still permeated with the dread of thirst, as illustrated by the words of the prophet Hosea:

"...I will strip her naked and leave her as on the day she was born. And **I will make her like a desert**, render her like a parched land **and let her die of thirst**." (Hosea 2:5)

And some 150 years after Hosea, the prophet Ezekiel expresses himself in like manner:

"Your mother was like a vine...planted beside water, with luxuriant boughs and branches thanks to abundant water...**Now she is planted in the**

desert, in ground that is arid and parched."

(Ezekiel 19:10,13)

This wording may seem anachronistic because Ezekiel, sent into exile by Nebuchadnezzar, prophesied while living among the exiles in Babylon on the banks of the Euphrates River. Yet the prophet still speaks of his immediate reality not as the "abundant water" of Babylon, but the dryness of the desert!

Thirst in the desert is evoked in many other places in the Bible in different words:

> "A psalm of **David** when he was **in the Judean Desert**: God, You are my God; I search for You, **my soul thirsts for You**, my body yearns for You, **in a parched and thirsty land that has no water.**"
>
> (Psalm 63:1-2)

David, of course, experienced the Judean Desert in his youth when he pastured his fathers flocks, and later when he was pursued by Saul, and later still when he fled from his son Absalom. It is not surprising, therefore, that the desert haunts several psalms bearing David's name. Even if David himself was not the poet, whoever was must have experienced desert life before attributing poems to David "when he was in the Judean Desert."

Because water is the most important ingredient for life in the desert, the words for thirst and tiredness are frequently used synonymously in the Bible. Anyone who has experienced the desert knows that one of the first warnings of dehydration is general fatigue.

Sources of water in the desert

There are five sources of water in the desert. Three of them — rainwater, water holes, and springs — are natural. The other two, wells and cisterns, have to be hewn, dug, or built before they will hold water. Both categories are found in Biblical and Talmudic sources.

As everyone knows, rainfall in the desert is minimal, averaging from less than 100 mm (4 inches) to 350 mm (14 inches). While this is insufficient for productive agriculture, it

not only on the common knowledge that the oleander is bitter and poisonous, but also on the fact that it always grows near water. The idea of bitter healing bitter brings to mind vaccinations as well as some of the compounds used in homeopathic medicine.

(*) **Rabbi Yehoshua ben Korha** — fourth generation of *tannaim* (135-170 CE).

57

7. Jacob's blessing over Judah

"His eyes are darker than wine; his teeth are whiter than milk."   (Genesis 49:12)

These words in Jacob's blessing of his son, Judah, describe the land allotted to that tribe where the grape growers lived side by side with the shepherds in the desert borderlands just as they obviously did in the days of King Uzziah.

8. The "ring" of the cistern and the hungry lion

The photograph on the *right* in the foreground clearly shows a round, stone "ring" two-thirds of the way down the slope in the Judean Desert. This stone ring is placed on the mouth of a deep, bell-shaped cistern cut in bedrock and usually plastered with lime to prevent seepage; the ring eases the chaffing on

is more than adequate for wide areas of pastureland to become green during the winter months and provide water for those perennial shrubs that can survive in years of drought. Because desert rainfall is erratic, desert plants often concentrate primarily in those places were there is water runoff from a wide area. This gives desert plants access to significantly more water than is measured by annual rainfall. The reverse also holds true: there are many plants, especially annuals, that are unable to utilize even that minimal rain that does come their way, because after the topsoil level is saturated, the water does not penetrate deeper into the soil. It flows into the wadis, and some remains in rock hollows and natural pools that form in the rockbeds of the watercourses. These are the water holes, which, depending on their capacity, hold water in good years not only during the rainy season but throughout the dry summer. Indeed, some water holes can retain rainwater from an exceptionally wet year clear through the following year, even if there are no rains in the second year to refill them. If the winter rains are heavy and the floods in the wadis are strong and frequent, the water in the water holes will be fresher and more potable. Water holes serve not only people in the desert, but also all the animals who quench their thirst at these precious points.

Obviously, people learned from nature. If floodwaters normally collect in natural water holes, why not direct the water to pools and cisterns hand-hewn along the banks of dry river beds or on the slopes of hills? According to archaeologists, hewing cisterns in the mountainous and border desert regions, and plastering and sealing them were skills developed by the Israelites as early as the entry into the Promised Land under Joshua in the 13th century BCE. Later, this is related concerning Uzziah, King of Judah:

> "He built **towers in the desert** and **hewed out many cisterns**, for he had many herds, and farmers in the foothills and on the plain, and grape growers in the hills and on the Carmel, for he loved the soil." [7] (II Chronicles 26:10)

That King Uzziah hewed out the cisterns [8] in the desert

the rope attached to the jug or bucket used to draw water from the cistern. The photograph also shows remnants of conduits that channeled precious rainwater from the surrounding hills *(left)*. As a slow desert shower fast turns into a downpour, rivulets of water quickly start to flow down the bare hills and into the conduits carefully constructed to direct the flow to the opening **below** the stone ring. This image was used by the Elders of Israel who came to King David to inform him of the people's economic distress: "Your people Israel need a livelihood. To which David replied: Let them earn a living by trading with one another. The Sages answered: **A mouthful cannot satisfy a lion, nor can a cistern fill up from its ring.**" (Brakhot 3b) Clearly, a cistern cannot fill up only from the rain that falls directly into

because "he had many herds" emphasizes that **the amount of drinking water is no less a limiting factor on the number of flocks that can graze in the desert than the quantity of grazing land available there.**

Churned up springs and spoiled water sources

Should the current in a wadi not be strong enough to scour out the bottom of the water hole, sediment will accumulate and occasionally algae will develop. Such water is less potable, and out of consideration for others who may need it later, care should be taken to disturb the sediment and impurities as little as possible.

> "Is it not enough for you to graze on choice grazing ground, but you must also trample with your feet what is left from your grazing? You drink clear water [water that has settled] but you also muddy with your feet what is left! And My flock graze on what your feet have trampled and drink what your feet have muddied!" (Ezekiel 34: 18-19)

I clearly remember an incident when "water discipline" was

strictly enforced in the days of Haganah and Palmach training. (Each person had two canteens of water a day during desert marches. We were permitted to drink from one; the other had to remain untouched for emergencies.) I was a field-craft instructor and arrived with my company at the Tze'elim wadi after many long, hot hours of exhausting walking from Ein Gedi along the shore of the Dead Sea. We were backpacking all our food and equipment for five days and nights. We climbed to the Anava spring, on the bank of one of the tributaries of the wadi. Drop by drop, the little spring fed water into a small pool and each member of the company drank in turn. In keeping with my training, I refrained from drinking until everyone else had quenched his thirst. As luck would have it, no one noticed that I had not yet enjoyed the clear, cold water, and some of the company quickly proceeded

its mouth; runoff from the entire drainage area must find its way into the cistern for it to be effective. By also using the example of the hungry lion that is not sated by a mere mouthful, the Elders reminded David of his shepherding experiences as a youth in the desert when he anxiously watched the flow of water into the cistern and had to protect his flocks from the marauding lions that came out of the Jordan thickets to appease their hunger by preying on the sheep and goats.

In contrast to a cistern, a **well** is dug into the ground until it hits groundwater. The difference between flowing water and

stored water enhanced the metaphoric language of the Bible. So says Jeremiah: "...Hew down her trees and raise siege ramps against Jerusalem...**As a well flows with water, so she flows with wickedness**...Learn your lesson, Jerusalem, lest...I leave you desolate, a land where no one can live."

(Jeremiah 6:6-8)

In this description, Jerusalem's evil flows from a source that does not cease to produce fresh evil — a well that is nurtured from underground waters, not those collected from runoff water. Proverbs (18:4) uses the same metaphor

to remove their boots and thrust their feet into the last of the water remaining in the little pool. The water was instantly muddied and fouled to such a degree that, despite my intense thirst, I could not drink from it. In those exceedingly difficult moments, the first words that came to mind were:

"Cold water to a parched throat — good news from a distant land. A **churned up spring**, a spoiled water source — a righteous man fallen before a wicked one." [9]   (Proverbs 25:25-26)

More than 24 additional hours passed before I was able to quench my thirst. It was when we reached Ein Bokek the next evening after a day of walking from Masada in the "broken land" formation of glaring, salty hills. Before nightfall, as we passed from the shore of the Dead Sea to the dark canyon, suddenly we heard the great miracle: the delectable song of running water! Together with the rest of the company, I plunged fully dressed into the middle of the current and drank, and drank, and drank...and drank again, and paddled around in the water, and drank again...and then, suddenly the sound of water splashing and gurgling in utter darkness called to mind the words of the prophet Jeremiah:

> "'For I will give the thirsty abundant drink, and satisfy all who languish.' At this I awoke and looked about, and my sleep had been satisfying."
>
> (Jeremiah 31:24-25)

Indeed the prophet was right. After the exhaustion from thirst had passed when I quenched my thirst, I slept deeply that night, completely sated. I have experienced nothing similar but to a different purpose:

"The words a man speaks are deep waters; [but] a flowing stream is the fount of wisdom."

The proverb can be reworded like this: Rhetoric is like deep water in a cistern that has nothing of its own, nothing original. Wisdom, on the other hand, is original and flows as a stream from the wellspring.

9. The righteous cannot die before the wicked!

The author of the following homily obviously never experienced what is described in Proverbs (25:25-26), because he explains the verses in a different light:

"Rabbi Yehuda: [*] Just as it is impossible for a wellspring to be muddied or for a spring to be corrupted, so it is impossible for a righteous man to die before the wicked one." (Breshit Rabbah 75b) This optimistic exposition obviously refers to the actual source from which clear water constantly flows and not to the storage reservoir that may be built beside the spring.

[*] **Rabbi Yehuda (ben Shimon ben Pazi)** – first generation *amora* in Israel (220-250 CE).

10. Ein Prat, Ephrat and Rachel's burial place

The matter of Ein Prat and Jeremiah cannot be completed without relating to the problem of Rachel's burial place.

"Thus said the Lord: A cry is heard in Ramah, wailing, bitter weeping, Rachel weeping for her children. She refuses to be comforted for her children, who are gone." (Jeremiah 31:14)

In my first book, *New Light on the Book of Jeremiah*, I dealt with the puzzle of Rachel's burial place. What follows is a slightly edited and abbreviated version of this thesis.

From Jeremiah's lamentation it is obvious that the place of Rachel's burial was known to Jeremiah as near Ramah (considered almost unanimously by scholars to be in the vicinity of the Arab town A-Ram, some nine km north of Jerusalem). From I Samuel (10:2) it is also clear that Rachel's burial place was somewhere close to Ramah or to Gibeah (two-and-a-half km east of Ramah), but certainly within the boundaries of the land allotted to the tribe of Benjamin: "When you [Saul] leave me [Samuel] today, you will meet two men near the tomb of Rachel **in the territory of Benjamin, at Tzeltzakh.**"

since. The next morning I felt totally refreshed and ready for another day of hiking in the desert heat.

Broken cisterns

"For My people have done a twofold evil: they have forsaken Me, the Fount of living waters, and hewed them out cisterns, broken cisterns, which cannot even hold water." (Jeremiah 2:13)

These words recall something worthy of attention: In Anatot, Jeremiah's birthplace located on the edge of the desert, northeast of Jerusalem, there is not a single spring, not even in the immediate vicinity. Neither are there any springs in neighboring villages.

Here were five adjacent ancient villages in the land of Benjamin on the edge of the desert, and not a spring among them! On the other hand, these villages had numerous cisterns where winter runoff water collected. Cisterns can only substitute for a spring; they are not the perfect replacement. In a year of little rain, the cisterns fill only partially, and their level steadily sinks as the water is used, until the hardship becomes unbearable.

In Tekoa, the hometown of the prophet Amos, south of Jerusalem and also on the edge of the desert, a similar situation prevails: there is no spring in the vicinity and the only sources of water are the hewn-out cisterns that collect winter runoff. This is what Amos said of drought: "Two or three towns would wander to a single town to drink water, but their thirst would not be slaked..." (Amos 4:8) This was a description drawn from events Amos must have experienced several times: when their cisterns ran dry, people from a settlement with no spring had to get drinking water from distant settlements close to year-round sources of water. This reality was being experienced in drought years in the area of Jerusalem even at the time of the establishment of the modern State of Israel in 1948.

I remember an incident in the winter of 1946-47, an extremely dry year, when the hiking group I led reached the village of Abu Dis east of Jerusalem after a long night of climbing by moonlight from the shores of the Dead Sea near Ein Feshkha and all the way across the desert. We were exhausted and parched, but the inhabitants of the village apologized for their inability to give us water because their cisterns were dry and the water carriers who went to the spring at Shiloah (a distance of eight km there and back) had not yet returned.

No doubt Jeremiah was witness to such situations, and one can suppose that he was sent to the distant spring in hard times when the cisterns of Anatot were empty. There is a spring about eleven km round-trip from Anatot, the return route being a long, steep ascent. The large spring, gushing water even in the driest years, is called Ein Fara in Arabic. The latest hiker's map of the National Trail Marking Committee has restored to the spring its Biblical name, *Ein Prat*.[10] The spring is located in the deep chasm of Nahal Prat, and near it is a ruin called by the Arabs "the tel" or the "Ruin of Ein Prat," evidently the Parah mentioned as one of the towns of Benjamin in the book of Joshua (18:23). In *New Light on the Book of Jeremiah*, I suggested that this was the Ephrat that Rachel and Jacob were trying to reach when she died giving birth to Benjamin.

Zechariah Kalai, in *Judaea, Samaria and the Golan — Archaeological Survey 1967-1968*, p. 185 (Jerusalem, 1972), describes the pottery finds in this location: "Those found in the tel and the terraces are from the early Canaanite period [Early Bronze, 3150-2200 BCE]. Those near the remains of the dam, are from the Roman, Byzantine and Arab periods [first through seventh centuries CE]." The results of this survey thus indicate that, although this site was inhabited during the Canaanite period, it was deserted during Jeremiah's time. Surely Jeremiah must have repeatedly asked himself: why was such a perfect location abandoned by its inhabitants? And why were Anatot and her sister settlements built so far away from this reliable source of water? What was the point of settling in a place where cisterns had to be hewn, especially in this desert border area, instead of settling and developing the area around the bountiful spring — and enjoying it? Certainly these questions must have bothered Jeremiah, especially during the weary climbs behind the donkey carrying the

However, these two references in Jeremiah and Samuel seem to contradict what is recounted in Genesis: "They set out from Bethel; but when they were just some distance short of Ephrat, Rachel was in childbirth, and she had hard labor...Thus Rachel died. She was buried on the road to **Ephrat — now Bethlehem**." (35:16,19) "When I [Jacob] was returning from Paddan, Rachel died while I was journeying in the land of Canaan, when still some distance short of **Ephrat**; and I buried her there on the road to **Ephrat — now Bethlehem**." (48:7) In fact, a relatively late tradition places "Rachel's Tomb" at the entrance to today's Bethlehem. But Bethlehem, as everyone knows, is located **south of Jerusalem**, in the land allotted to the tribe of Judah, not north of Jerusalem in the land of Benjamin!

This apparent contradiction caused a lot of debate concerning the identification of Rachel's burial place.

On one of my frequent hikes in the territory of Benjamin, during a hot summer day, it occurred to me that the "Ephrat — now Bethlehem" mentioned in Genesis is not the Bethlehem in Judah [the town of Jesus' birth] but **another Bethlehem somewhere in the land of Benjamin**. If I could find this other Bethlehem, at least part of the problem would be solved. That day, the trail took me to the gushing spring in the cool, lush canyon of Ein Prat. Suddenly it clicked in my mind that the Arabic name, Prat, was a slight corruption of the name of the ancient Ephrat, which was Jeremiah's "Prat" where he hid his loincloth (Jeremiah 13:4-7)! In the book of Joshua (18:23), a "Parah" mentioned in the list of the villages of Benjamin is considered by most scholars to have been located adjacent to the spring of Ein Prat. It is almost inevitable that in ancient times the area around the spring was populated, fruitful, and probably a center of the territories that later fell to Benjamin and Judah.

Jacob traveled south from Bethel . The most comfortable road was determined not only by topography but primarily by the availability of water and the proximity to settlements. Bearing this in mind, Jacob's route must have taken him a bit to the east of the mountain ridge, to the famous spring and oasis of Prat and from there ascended south.

The name Ephrat is similar to the Arabic name Ein Prat and also to Joshua's Parah. But where does Bethlehem fit in? The book of Genesis emphasizes twice that Ephrat is "now Bethlehem" (meaning that by the time this story was written, the name Ephrat had already been changed to Bethlehem.) In fact we find confirmation of this supposition in the book of Nehemiah, in the listing of the returnees from the villages of Benjamin: "the sons of Gibeon — 95; **the men of Bethlehem** and Netophah — 188; the men of Anatot — 128; the men of Bet-A'zmavet — 42." (Nehemiah 7:25-28) Here Bethlehem replaces Parah, which is mentioned in Joshua 18:23 among the same villages of Benjamin. It seems to me that both appellations are in fact different names with the same meaning. The famous Euphrates in Babylon is called in Hebrew Prat פרת, because of its fertility (*poriut* פוריות). It is a logical meaning because the environs of that river were famous for their fruit. The same can be said about the meaning of Prat and Parah located as they were on the largest spring in the territory of Benjamin. And Bethlehem has the same meaning: "the house of bread" or "the

waterskins and jugs from the spring during his childhood and youth. How natural that this mystery should make its way in the form of a parable into Jeremiah's anguished plea that the people return to follow the one true God, the source of all life, leaving the false and empty gods: **"They have forsaken Me, the Fount of living waters, and hewed them out cisterns, broken cisterns, which cannot even hold water."** (Jeremiah 2:13)

In this parable, two wrongs are underscored — "twofold evil": not only have the people forsaken the spring of living water, they hewed cisterns in the wrong kind of rock; if there are cracks in the rock, then the cisterns too will be "broken" and unable to hold the water that flows into them.

The spring of Ein Prat **opposite page**: *Ruins of ancient Ephrat*

"A tree planted by water" vs. the "Sodom apple in the wilderness"

Jeremiah relates what happened to him on his way to Prat:

> "Thus the Lord said to me: Go buy yourself a loincloth of linen, and put it around your loins, but do not dip it into water. So I bought the loincloth in accordance with the Lord's command, and put it about my loins. And the word of the Lord came to me a second time: Take the loincloth which you bought, which is about your loins, and go to Prat and cover it up there in a cleft of the rock. I went and buried it at Prat, as the Lord had commanded me. Then, after a long time, the Lord said to me: Go to Prat and take there the loincloth which I commanded you to bury there. So I went to Prat and dug up the loincloth from the place where I had buried it and found the loincloth ruined; it was not good for anything. The word of the Lord came to me: Thus said the Lord: Even so will I ruin the overweening pride of Judah and Jerusalem...[they] shall become like that loincloth, which is not good for anything."
>
> (Jeremiah 13:1-10)

Even today, if we place in a rock crevice in Ein Prat any object made from organic material (such as a linen belt or the loincloth, mentioned by Jeremiah), it will decompose because of the moisture that collects in every fissure and rock depression above the spring. But the high humidity and the heavy shade cast by the high canyon walls during most daylight hours create ideal conditions for the trees that grow here. The relative coolness of this place is remarkable in contrast to the heat of the surrounding desert. A memorable pleasure on a scorching day is to go down to Ein Prat, enjoy the cool shade beside the plentiful water, and relish the fruit of the fig trees that grow there along the stream bed. In such a moment every word of Jeremiah's metaphor is clearly felt:

> "Blessed is he who trusts in the Lord, whose trust is the Lord alone. He shall be like a tree planted by waters, sending forth its roots by a stream. It does

house of fertility." Therefore, it is not unreasonable that Ephrat ("fertility"), famous for its fruit, would also be called Bethlehem, the house of bread. (Nor is it surprising that the Bethlehem in Judah was also called "Ephrat." Even today the Judean Bethlehem is famous for its wonderful olives and for its lush fields spreading east, unequaled in the Judean hills.)

From everything mentioned so far, one can conclude that the "Ephrat — now Bethlehem" of Genesis was an ancient town built near the spring of Ein Prat, famous as a regional center before the rise of Jerusalem. It may also be possible that at first it was called "Ephrat" and only later "Bethlehem," which would explain why this point had to be made twice in Genesis. After all, while in the book of Joshua it is called "Parah," in the book of Nehemiah (some 600 years later) the same place is called Bethlehem.

Now that the location of this "Ephrat" is reasonably ascertained, it can help us locate the burial place of Rachel. The road from Bethel to Ephrat passes between Ramah and Gibeah before descending into the wadi southwards and twisting with the wadi till it comes to the spring of Ein Prat. On the descent from Gibeah, just where the wadi turns east, after the greatest part of the distance from Bethel has been covered and only a relatively short walk remains to the Prat spring, the traveler suddenly comes to five large stone structures which the Arabs call *Kub'r B'nai Yisrael,* "the graves of the Children of Israel." Researchers are puzzled by these structures; some have suggested that they are megalithic (2000-1500 BCE, which covers the period of the patriarchs). The Arabs do not know why their tradition has given these structures such a peculiar name. I am raising the possibility that they are a piece in the puzzle of the location of Rachel's tomb, for they are exactly "but a short distance from Ephrat" for someone going from Bethel to Ein Prat.

Jacob, with Rachel in the last stages of pregnancy, is traveling south from Bethel. According to his calculations, he should easily be able to reach the idyllic Ephrat that same day. That is where Rachel will give birth to their child and rest in the shade of the fruit trees, enjoying the coolness of the spring. But suddenly, a short way from Ephrat, just an hour's donkey ride from the spring, Rachel goes into labor in an arid place with no water, and there she dies. The child born was Benjamin, the only son born to Jacob in the Land of Israel, and the territory allotted to his descendants was the area of his birth, including "Ephrat now Bethlehem."

Jacob built a memorial worthy of Rachel, his best-loved wife, not far from E p h r a t **inside** the boundary of Benjamin (not "on" the boundary) which is "the memorial to Rachel's burial place till today." (Genesis 35:20) If we accept the thesis that *Kub'r B'nai Yisrael* is indeed associated with Rachel's death,

not fear the coming of heat, its leaves are ever fresh. It has no care in a year of drought; it does not cease to yield fruit." (Jeremiah 17:7-8)

Indeed, the fig trees growing here as they do near other desert springs and streams are not affected either by the heat that beats down on the hills above the spring or by the cold of winter, as are the figs growing in lush hill areas. As a result, instead of shedding their leaves in winter as fig trees normally do, the fig trees growing in Ein Prat are leafy almost year round and even give fruit for most of the year (instead of during the normal season from late May to September only). But as soon as you climb up out of the shady, wet chasm in the direction of Anatot, you are smitten by the heat as with a physical blow. If you look left, to the east, you can see in the distance the wilderness of Jericho shimmering in the sun, mottled with patches of green against the light yellow of the naked saltlands. There, far away, between the Dead Sea and Jericho, grows the "cursed lemon of the wilderness," the *a'ra'r* ערער, which represented to Jeremiah the diametric opposite of the "tree planted by waters":

"Cursed is he who trusts in man, who makes mere flesh his strength, and turns his thoughts from the

68   *Kub'r B'nai Yisrael - is this where Jacob buried Rachel? birth to Benjamin?*   **opposite page**: *Is this Tzeltzakh ("Dry Shade") where Rachel gave*

Lord. He shall be like the **a'ra'r in the wilderness**, which does not sense the coming of good: It is set in the scorched places of the desert, in a salty land without inhabitant."

(Jeremiah 17:5-6)

The "cursed *a'ra'r*" in the wilderness is also found in "a prayer of the lowly man when he is faint and pours forth his plea before the Lord" (Psalm 102:1):

"You will surely arise and take pity on Zion, for it is time to be gracious to her; the appointed time has come. Your servants take delight in its stones, and cherish its dust. The nations will fear the name of the Lord, all the kings of the earth, Your glory. For

all the questions and discrepancies concerning Rachel's burial place will be solved, together with an explanation of the strange name given by the Arabs to the ancient "graves." These are the "graves" of the Children of Israel who buried the matriarch Rachel here and came to the grave occasionally to pray.

But we still have to identify **"Tzeltzakh"** צלצח. In this case too, the commentators had trouble identifying an exact location and suggested instead different "corrections" to solve the difficulty. A distance of five minutes walk from these ancient "graves" stands a large cliff facing north-northeast, on the ascent to Gibeah. It casts a deep shade during most daylight hours. In Hebrew the word for shade is...*tzel* צל. Just a little further are the cliffs of the Prat spring, also facing north, also casting heavy shade, but with the incomparable accompaniment of gurgling water at their base. But under the cliff first mentioned there is not a drop of water, all is utterly dry. What is the Hebrew word for arid or dry? *tzakh* צח! Is it not logical that the Israelites called this place "Arid Shade" — Tzeltzakh – צלצח in diametric contrast to the water-rich shade so close by, the spring of Prat?

It is clear why Saul, the young man of the tribe of Benjamin, on the great day that he was anointed king of Israel by the prophet Samuel (I Samuel 10:1) would make a very small detour to Tzeltzakh on his way from Ramah to Gibeah. Tzeltzakh was the burial place of his tribe's mother, the matriarch of the nation; it was natural that he wanted to pray at her tomb on this most fateful day of his life.

This also clears up Jeremiah's geographic reference to Ramah. These ancient "graves" are located at the foot of the slope on which Ramah was situated, hence his words, "A cry is heard in Ramah."

I was happy to find the following tanta-lizing confirmation in support of my theory. Clermont-Ganneau, one of the first archaeologists to work in this region, wrote in an article published in *Archaeological Researches in Palestine* 1873-74, Vol II. p. 278: "For reasons I cannot go into, I will show that here [at *Kub'r B'nai Yisrael*] is the true location of Rachel's tomb. This supposition may seem very daring. One day I will certainly expand my writing on this subject without avoiding the various difficulties inherent in this idea."

the Lord has built Zion; He has appeared in all His glory. He has turned to the prayer of the *a'ra'r* and has not spurned their prayer." (Psalm 102:14-18)

Hannah and Ephraim Hareuveni, in their article, *Ha-a'ra'r* ("Magnes Book" Hebrew University Press, 1938), presented the results of their long and detailed research, concluding that the *a'ra'r* mentioned in the book of Jeremiah and the psalms is the tree *Calotropis procera*, also known today as the Sodom apple. According to the Bedouin tribe studied by the Hareuvenis in the wilderness of Jericho, the tree is cursed

from the days of Sodom and Gommorah which is why they call it the "cursed lemon." Its fruit is large and attracts the eye by its wholesome appearance, but it contains only desiccated, silken "threads" that serve as "parachutes" for the dry, brown seeds. Once, say the Bedouin, in the days of "Master Lot," the fruit was juicy and refreshing. But when men sinned and were punished with the curse of Sodom and Gommorah, this fruit was cursed with them. When mankind repents of its evil ways, the fruit of the cursed lemon will be cleansed and its juice will be as delicious and satisfying as it was before the destruction of Sodom and Gommorah. In the above-mentioned article, the Hareuvenis give several similar examples from the homilies of the Sages. For instance, Rabbi Oshaya[11] (Yoma 21,2) tells of the wondrous golden trees that Solomon planted in the Temple courtyard. When enemies entered the Temple, the trees stopped giving fruit and withered away, "but the Lord shall return them."

This cursed *a'ra'r* appears to stand in the arid and salty wilderness spreading its "palms" in prayer. Its broad leaves appear like upturned hands. When the psalmist describes the redemption of Zion from its ruin, he sees it in the form of the *a'ra'r* praying for redemption like "the lowly man when he is faint and pours forth his plea before the Lord," and God in His infinite mercy does "not spurn their prayer."

Unfortunately, nowhere was I able to find any further reference by Clermont-Ganneau to Rachel's tomb, so I must assume that he never published his full explanation. However, I did find that Macalister agreed with Clermont-Ganneau's theory but that he too did not explain his reasons for accepting it.

11. Rabbi Oshaya (or Hoshaya) one of the greatest Sages in Israel during the transitional period between the *tannaim* and the *amoraim* (200-220 CE).

Jeremiah, on the other hand, does not appeal for mercy to rehabilitate the *a'ra'r*. On the contrary, while the tree planted by waters will "not cease to yield fruit," representing the reward of the person who trusts in God, the *a'ra'r* symbolizes the curse of dryness that will fall upon "the man who makes mere flesh his strength."

"They came to the water holes but found no water."

Every fluctuation of rainfall or change in its frequency during the rainy season is magnified in the desert several times more strongly than in the mountainous regions, which receive fair amounts of rain. Even in the borderline desert area, which includes Biblical Jerusalem [12] as well as Anatot and Tekoa, the home villages of Jeremiah and Amos, the annual fluctuations in the amount of rainfall affect the crops much more severely than in the mountain regions. The less rainfall there is, the more crucial is its distribution to the success of the crops over the five months of the rainy season (November to March). In some years the continuous drought in these areas is so severe that the intervals between rains lose significance, and the only prayer remaining is for rain to come, even if it is in one single, drenching downpour. Although such a cloudburst will not save the sown fields, at least it will partially fill the water holes in the desert stream beds, and in the borderline desert settlements somewhat replenish the reserves in cisterns and reservoirs with drinking water for people and animals. This is how Jeremiah describes the drought:

12. Zion and Jerusalem

It is important to distinguish between modern Jerusalem, spreading widely over the mountains of the Mediterranean region, and Biblical Jerusalem, whose "roots" were in the City of David opposite the village of Shiloah and whose "branches" rose in the direction of the Temple Mount and the areas north and west of it. The ancient city is close to the Judean Desert, and should be counted among the borderline desert cities. Even the other name for Jerusalem, Zion — *tziyon* ציון — attests to its proximity to the desert, the dry place — *tziya* ציה.

"The word of the Lord which came to Jeremiah concerning the droughts: Judah is in mourning, her settlements languish; men sink to the ground, **and Jerusalem's cry rises**. The masters sent the boys for water; they came to the water holes but found no water there. They returned with empty vessels; they were shamed and humiliated, they bowed their heads. The soil is cracked because there is no rain. The farmers are shamed, they bow their heads in grief. Even the doe in the field forsook her newborn fawn because there was no grass. And the wild horses stood on the bare heights snuffing the air like owls; their eyes failed because there was no food."

(Jeremiah 14:1-6)

13. The doe in the field and the wild horses on the bare heights

It is characteristic of Jeremiah's faithful accuracy about the natural world that these two specific animals appear in his depiction of the tragic consequences of drought on the desert borders. The "doe in the field" represents those animals that live in the western regions of the desert (borderline desert), while the wild horses live in the deep desert. But they too must drink water at least once every two days. In desperation they stood on

Despite Jeremiah's poignant and accurate descriptions [13], Bible critics and commentators did not understand the verses' appalling significance, because as readers they were completely removed from the distinctive geographical and climatic features of Jerusalem and its environs. A number of commentators explained that the "masters" were really the "nobles" of Jerusalem and the "boys" were "servants" sent to fetch water from Jerusalem's own cisterns, only to find them dry. But how could this be? All of Jerusalem's public water resources, including the Gihon Spring, were insufficient for the total needs of the city's constantly growing population. For this reason, throughout Jerusalem's history, each house had its own cistern to catch rain runoff. Usually the water in these cisterns was sufficient for the residents' year-round needs. (These "home cisterns" were an integral part of Jerusalem's water supply until the construction in the latter years of the British mandate of the system which brought water to Jerusalem from the Yarkon springs in Rosh Ha'ayin located some 60 km away in the coastal plain. [14]) The home cisterns caught every possible drop of water that fell on the rooftops and in the courtyards during the rainy season. If the year showed signs of being water-poor, Jerusalem householders started rationing water. If a cistern ran dry, every person in the neighborhood knew it. It is inconceivable that in such an event, the entire city — including the highest nobles — not know of the water situation. No one had to wait for the "servants to return from the cisterns" to learn that they were empty. It is far more likely that the boys were sent out along the desert border and back to Jerusalem to bring water from the spring of Prat, a round trip of some 25 km. (In modern times the British Mandate government laid pipes and pumped water from Ein Prat up to Jerusalem. This pipeline operated throughout the 19 years of Jordanian occupation of East Jerusalem and ceased only when the Old City of Jerusalem was connected up to the National Water Carrier system of the State of Israel in 1967.)

But Jeremiah's description clearly reveals that even the spring of Prat did not always save the situation in Jerusalem — "and Jerusalem's cry rises." Perhaps the use of the word "droughts" in the first verse, in the plural, is an indication that

Jeremiah was describing events during a period of prolonged drought that lasted for more than one rainless winter. Such extended droughts are not uncommon in Israel, one of the more notable having occurred during the reign of King David when there was drought — and the consequent famine — "year after year for three years." (II Samuel 21:1) Indeed the description of this catastrophe reveals suffering far greater than that experienced in a "normal" drought. When the drought is prolonged, many springs run dry and even a large and normally gushing spring such as the Prat is reduced to a trickle. Such is the tragedy that Jeremiah describes:

> "Why must my pain be endless, my wound incurable, resistant to healing? You have been to me like **a spring that fails, like waters that cannot be trusted.**" [15]   (Jeremiah 15:18)

In those days the immediate consequence would have been the refusal of people from the surrounding area to give the boys ready access to whatever precious water was available. The same situation was probably true of the two other springs that emanate below the Prat spring, Ein Fuar and Ein Kelt. These springs flow down to Jericho where they irrigate the groves and fields; they certainly were not freely accessible to the people of Jerusalem, especially during a period such as the one Jeremiah describes.

the bare heights and snuffed the air to cool their bodies.

Israel Aharoni, modern Israel's first zoologist, wrote in his autobiography, *Memoirs of a Hebrew Zoologist* (Am Oved, 1936, p. 106): "The *pe're* פרא is thought of as a wild ass but it is, in fact, **a small horse...**[onager, *Equus hemionus*) It has a huge head, mostly taken up by nostrils. I have never seen such enormous and wide nostrils on any other animal in the world...When I saw its nostrils, I realized that they could inhale a great deal of air into its lungs and that this thin-legged, fine-figured creature could gallop with ease for many hours and never empty its lungs of air because of the extraordinary "pump" with which it is equipped! Seeing its nostrils, I understood the wonderful passage in Jeremiah (14:6): 'And the wild horses stand on the bare heights, snuffing the air like *tanim* תנים.' (*Tanim* are large desert owls, which gulp air to inflate their bodies and so frighten their enemies [by appearing to be larger than actual size]." (I had the privilege to study under Israel Aharoni 50 years ago when I was a student at the Hebrew University in Jerusalem.)

14. The cisterns that saved Jerusalem in 1948

Veteran residents of Jerusalem will never forget the home cisterns' crucial role in saving them from grave water shortages during the siege in the 1948 War of Independence. Many casualties occurred as residents left their homes to draw water from the cisterns in the courtyards and were exposed to the artillery fire relentlessly poured on Jerusalem by the Jordanian forces of the Arab Legion.

15. "You shall be...like a spring whose waters do not fail."
In marked contrast to Jeremiah's "spring that fails," and "waters that cannot be trusted" is Isaiah's metaphor:

"The Lord will guide you always; He will slake your thirst in parched places and give strength to your bones. You shall be like a watered garden, like a spring whose waters do not lie."

(Isaiah 58:11)

Still, the emphasis on "a spring whose waters do not lie" implies that there are springs whose waters **do** lie, i.e., fail.

16. Labor problems in the rebuilding of Jerusalem
The masters of the flock — *adirei hatzon* אדירי הצאן — are mentioned by Nahum (3:18): "Your shepherds are slumbering, O king of Assyria; Your masters of the flock are asleep." In Nehemiah (3:5) the same word, *adir* אדיר, appears: "...the Tekoites worked, though their masters (*adirehem* אדיריהם) would not take upon their shoulders the work of their lords." This statement caused commentators endless puzzlement because they did not realize that here too the word *adir* means "**flock** master," not simply "master." Assuming this, it is easy to understand that although the people of Tekoa helped build "the Fish Gate" (of Jerusalem) (Nehemiah 3:3), their flock masters refused to work under the lords (remember that Tekoa was a borderline

The only hope of finding water in such years of drought was, of all places, in the dry desert stream beds. Even in the driest of years, the heavens will suddenly open over a small area in the mountains or on the edge of the desert and a cloudburst will release relatively large quantities of water in a very short time. This rainwater will immediately flow east in the wadis, into the Dead Sea, but significant amounts will be trapped in the water holes of the stream beds. The largest water holes, which can contain truly impressive quantities of water, are usually found in the eastern part of the desert, deep in the shaded canyons near the mouths of the wadis. Neither the Jerusalem nobles nor their servants could get to these desert water holes. As spoiled city dwellers, they could not withstand the formidable hardships of the long journey, especially with no drinking water on the way. Moreover, they did not have the desert skill to find the right places.

This is why Jeremiah follows "the cry of Jerusalem" with the mention of the masters who sent the shepherd boys for water, but who found no water in the water holes and had to return with empty vessels... (Jeremiah 14:3) The **"masters"** are the flock-masters, **the owners of the sheep and goats,** [16] who sent their **shepherd boys** for water, and not "nobles" as appears in the Jewish Publication Society translation.

Jeremiah refers to these masters of the flock in another prophecy:

"Howl, you shepherds, and yell. Strew [dust] on yourselves, you **masters of the flock**! For the day of your slaughter draws near...Flight shall fail the shepherds, and escape, the **masters of the flock**! Hark, the outcry of the shepherds and the howls of the **masters of the flock**! For the Lord is ravaging their pasture." (Jeremiah 25:34-36)

The "boys" who were sent for water are the **shepherd boys** of whom Jeremiah also speaks in his prophecies concerning the fate of Edom and Babylon:

"Hear then the plan which the Lord has devised against Edom and what He has purposed against the inhabitants of the south: surely the **shepherd**

boys shall drag them away." (Jeremiah 49:20)

"Hear then the plan that the Lord has devised against Babylon, and has purposed against the land of Chaldea: surely the **shepherd boys** shall drag them away." (Jeremiah 50:45)

desert town and its citizens were owners of flocks pastured in the desert). This exposition of *adirehem* אדיריהם can also clarify the reason for their refusal: it is reasonable to assume that the flock masters of Tekoa were insulted by the fact that "the Sheep Gate" was assigned to the priest, Eliashib, and to the men of Jericho (Nehemiah 3:1-2) and not to the "sheep-breeders from Tekoa" (Amos 1:1), and they expressed their protest by refusing to participate in the rebuilding of the Fish Gate!

Full water holes in the Judean Desert

17. Nothing to be ashamed of

Such disappointment was our lot during one of the Palmach's training marches conducted along the Dead Sea. That winter (1946-1947) had been unusually dry, yet we still hoped to find water in the water holes. Several times a number of us left the path and made our way up the wadis hoping to find usable water holes to which we could bring the whole

In light of this understanding of the terms **masters of the flock** and **shepherd boys** it is clear that in verse 14:3 Jeremiah is describing the shepherds' efforts to find filled water holes in distant, dry stream beds. The owners of the flocks sent the young shepherd boys there, for they were the ones most familiar with the desert trails and in the best physical condition to withstand the difficult, waterless journey. But even these almost superhuman efforts were to no avail: after the long, exhausting trek "they came to the water holes but found no water. They returned with empty vessels; they were shamed and humiliated, they bowed their heads." But why is the word "shamed" used? Surely it is utterly out of place here if it is understood to mean "ashamed." After all, there was no reason for the shepherd boys to be ashamed of

their journey. On the contrary, they did what they were entrusted to do with great courage and dedication, reaching the water holes despite the heat and dryness, and even managing to return and deliver the terrible news that their vessels were empty. In this case, as in several other places in the Bible, and especially in Jeremiah, it is possible to understand his use of the word *busha* בושה in the sense of "disappointment." [17] So too in the continuation of the verse: "The farmers are shamed, they bow their heads in grief." The farmer's land is dying of thirst, cracked and parched because of the lack of rain. All the farmer can feel is frustrated hopelessness, but he certainly had no reason for shame. His disappointment is so great that he too can only cover his face and weep.

"This wadi shall be full of pools."

The book of Kings tells of Jehoram, king of Israel, and Jehoshaphat, king of Judah, who decided to go to war against Moab and to get there by using "the road through the desert of Edom." (II Kings 3:8) To do that they naturally had to include the king of Edom in the exploit.

> "They marched for seven days until they rounded [the tip of the Dead Sea]; and there was no water left for the army or for the animals that were with them. 'Alas!' cried the king of Israel. 'The Lord has brought these three kings together only to deliver them into the hands of Moab'...[The prophet] Elisha said...'Thus said the Lord: This wadi shall be full of pools. For thus said the Lord: You shall see no wind, you shall see no rain, and yet the wadi shall be filled with water; and you and your herds and your pack animals shall drink'...And in the morning...water suddenly came from the direction of Edom and the land was covered with water.
>
> "Meanwhile, all the Moabites had heard that the kings were advancing to make war on them; every man old enough to bear arms rallied, and they stationed themselves at the border. Next morning,

company. But all the water holes disappointed us and repeatedly we returned with our "heads bowed," our containers empty, and with just one word on our tongues: "Nothing." Jeremiah's words floated in the air: "You have been to me like a spring that fails, like waters that cannot be relied on."   (Jeremiah 15:18)

Shame in the sense of disappointment can, I believe, be found in a number of places in the Bible. To give just a few examples:

"...You shall be put to shame through Egypt, just as you were put to shame through Assyria. From this way, too, you will come out with your hands clutching your head; for the Lord has rejected those you trust, from them you shall gain nothing."   (Jeremiah 2:36-37)

Clearly, here the Bible translator's use of "shame" is totally misleading. Jeremiah warns Israel not to trust Egypt because she shall **disappoint** Israel just as did Assyria. And vice versa:

"In You our fathers trusted; they trusted, and You rescued them. To You they

81

cried out and they escaped; in You they trusted and were not disappointed" (obviously not "put to shame" as translated by *The New English Bible*).

(Psalm 22:5-6)

Clearly, here too the psalmist is not speaking of shame; he asserts that one who is certain of God is not disappointed. And in Jeremiah:

"And Moab shall be disappointed ["shamed" in *The New English Bible*] because of Kemosh, as the House of Israel was disappointed ["shamed," *ibid.*] because of [the golden calves of] Bethel, on whom they relied."

(Jeremiah 48:13)

Perhaps there is also a connection between the Hebrew root for the word shame (*bosh* בוש) and the root of the word for dryness (*yavosh* יבש), just as a "disappointing" spring is one that has gone dry.

18. The battle topography

The event described in this account evidently took place in a wadi above the borders of Moab and Edom, at one of its bends in which the current flows southeast. The Moabites, who stood on the right bank of the wadi at the end of the bend, saw the wadi's length against the light of the rising winter sun in the southeast. The attacking army, which had already crossed the wadi at the bend curving west, was hidden by the shadow of the cliff, which the Moabites, blinded by the rays of the rising sun, could not see.

when they rose, the sun was shining over the water, and from the distance the water appeared to the Moabites as red as blood. 'That's blood!' they said. [18] 'The kings must have fought among themselves and killed each other. Now to the spoil, Moab!'"

(II Kings 3:9-23)

This story raises two problems. First of all, is it possible that Jehoram and Jehoshaphat decided to go to war taking "the road through the desert of Edom" without ascertaining the availability of water before starting out on such a long desert journey? Surely the commanders of the armies of Israel and Judah were experienced and familiar with the region's conditions! Such an oversight is inconceivable because the absence of water would ruin the campaign long before the clash of battle with Moab. Secondly, it is extremely strange that Edom joined in this war, even though Edom probably had sufficient reason to go to war against her neighbor to the north. More relevant was the deep hatred between Judea and Edom, dating back to the bloody war of David against Edom a hundred years earlier. One could suspect that, more than they wished to fight Moab, the Edomites wanted to use this opportunity to settle accounts with their bitter enemies, the descendants of David. So perhaps the Edomites gave the commanders of the army of Judea false information about the availability of water in the water holes in the region, while relying on sources of water known only to them for their own army's use. The Moabites' assumption that the armies of the three kings had started killing each other off, as the Bible relates, had obvious firm foundations.

Noisy pits and "malicious waters"

The same waters that give life in the desert may also take life in the desert when they reach it suddenly in raging torrents spilling down from the hills.

"...Of David:
Save me, O God, for the waters have risen up to my neck. I sink in muddy depths and have no foothold; I am swept into deep water, and the

torrent [*] carried me away...Let me be rescued from the mire, do not let me sink. Let me be rescued from my enemies and from the depth of the water. May the flood [*] not carry me away, nor the abyss swallow me up, nor the deep close over me."

(Psalm 69:2-3, 15-16)

The awesome sight of a desert wadi in full flood will do more for the understanding of this psalm than all the commentators and translators.

[*] The word used in the Hebrew Scriptures is *shibboleth* שיבולת, which means not only "torrent of water or flood" but also "ear of grain." The connection can be understood only by watching the rush of water in a rain-swollen wadi. Friction along the shoreline causes the water touching the banks of the stream to flow at a slower rate than the water in the center. The relatively faster flow in the center pulls towards it the slower-flowing waters, **creating wavelets that look like an ear of grain.** Such an "ear of water" is especially conspicuous when the current reaches a waterfall, its speed at the center increasing at a faster rate than the flow on the sides. The "ear of water" is, therefore, the most dangerous part of the stream, where the torrent is strongest. Anyone caught in such a turbulence has a better chance of escaping if he can get close to the bank, but if he is swept towards the center — to the "ear of water" — he has little chance of escaping before being pulled into the waterfall.

The force with which the falling water hits bottom frequently forms a deep pot hole which partially fills with silt. Often the current washes this silt out of the basin and deposits it just outside the rim of the pot hole, where it forms a loose, muddy barrier; this makes it extremely difficult to extricate oneself from the pot hole beneath the waterfall. This is exactly the fear voiced by David in psalm 69. In recent years there was at least one case, as far as I know, in which a hiker drowned in such a pot hole because he was unable to clamber over the silt barrier. A similar picture is found in another psalm bearing David's name:

"I put my hope in the Lord. He inclined toward me

83

and heeded my cry. He lifted me out of the roaring pit, the slimy clay, and set my feet on a rock, gave me firm footing." (Psalm 40:2-3)

The "roaring pit" caused confusion among commentators, who tried to explain it in outlandish ways — for what noise is there in a pit of water? Rashi described the "pit" as "the prison of Egypt," seeing this psalm (as did many of the Talmudic Sages) as representing the Children of Israel who were saved from the suffering of slavery in Egypt. The "pit" evidently reminded Rashi of the pit (dungeon) into which Joseph was thrown in Egypt after he was falsely accused by Potiphar's wife (Genesis 40:15); Rashi associated the roaring sound with the noise of the Red Sea as it closed over the armies of Egypt. But he totally ignored the source of the metaphor "the roaring pit." Modern Biblical critics suggested reading the phrase as "the pit of disaster" because of the similarity between the Hebrew word *shaon* שאון — thundering noise — and the word *shoah* שואה — disaster. (C. A. Briggs, vol. "Psalms," *International Critical Commentary*, Clark, Edinburgh, 1960, pp. 352, 358.)

The answer, as before, is found in the desert itself. The "roaring pit" is the pot hole carved out below the waterfall by the water as it hits bottom with great force and ear-splitting noise. There sediment borne along by the water is deposited, forming a "slimy clay." When you try to escape from the trap of such a pot hole walled in on three sides by steep cliffs, you seek every dubious foothold and grasp at the tiniest handhold in the cliff face. You continue to grope your way upward, heart in mouth, until at last you find your "feet set on a rock" and feel a sense of deep relief and reprieve to feel "firm footing" once again.

Another psalm bearing the name of David becomes vividly clear if the dangers of desert waters are real to the reader:

"A song...of David...Let Israel now declare: were it not for the Lord, Who was on our side when men assailed us, they would have swallowed us alive when their anger was roused against us. **The waters would have carried us off, the**

torrent would have swept over us, over us would have swept the malicious waters."

(Psalm 124:1-5)

In clear words and simple style the psalmist describes rescue from a trap set by a dangerous enemy, a trap that is quite naturally compared to the no less perilous flood in the wadi.

A barrier in the flood; shade in scorching heat

Waterfalls in the desert frequently create not only deep water holes but also small caves or clefts in the soft rock wall above the water hole, behind the falling curtain of water. Such clefts are also carved out in the bends of a wadi, especially where the rock walls are eroded by the racing waters of flash floods. These clefts provide shady niches during scorching summer days, particularly during the noon hours when neither the boulders nor the steep slopes cast shadows to provide shade. A little water left in the water hole from the last flood also helps alleviate the searing aridity. But this is only half the picture. If one is careless enough to be trapped in the wadi when he hears the roar of a flash flood thundering down from the heights, and the smooth sides of the canyon make quick escape impossible, he may be fortunate enough to find emergency refuge in such a "waterfall cave," should it be close at hand. The lucky traveler can then wait it out behind the cascading "drapery" and when the flow subsides just a few hours later, walk out intact, if sopping wet.

Such a shelter, providing refuge from the floods in winter and the searing sun in summer, is the only place that can be the natural setting for the following description:

> "For You have been a refuge for the poor man, a stronghold for the needy man in his distress, a shelter from the waterfall, a shade from the heat. For the fury of tyrants is like a roiling waterfall. You subdued the roaring of enemies with the dryness of the arid place; You subdued the dryness with heavy shade. The song of victory over the tyrants shall be sung." (Isaiah 25:4-5)

The fury of tyrants washes over the people with such

turbulence that it can destroy everything in its path, like that same roiling waterfall that drops with such noisy force over the face of the cliff. The Hebrew Scriptures use the word *shaon* שָׁאוֹן, which means roaring noise, to describe the tyrants who set the land awash with the noise of war. ("...the roar [*shaon*] of nations that roar as roar [*shaon*] the mighty waters." Isaiah 17:12) Just as in the end the arid land "subdues" the floodwaters, so shall the Lord subdue the "noise of strangers" who come to destroy Zion and Jerusalem. The words "You subdued the heat with heavy shade" can be appreciated by someone who has taken shelter in such a waterfall cave: after the dryness has "vanquished" the "roiling waterfall" and the intense heat has returned, the same cave provides blessed shade from the desert's merciless sun. There you can imagine David, safe from the elements, "addressing the words of this song to the Lord after the Lord had saved him from the hands of all his enemies and from the clutches of Saul" (Psalm 18:1):

> "O Lord, my crag, my fortress, my rescuer, my God, my rock in whom I seek refuge...Ropes of death encompassed me, currents of evil terrified me...He reached down from on high, He took me; He drew me out of the mighty waters." (Psalm 18:3, 5, 17)

This prayer of thanksgiving echoes the same feelings expressed in psalms 40 and 69: there God "lifted him out of the roaring pit"; in this psalm, "He reached down from on high...He drew me out of the mighty waters." There, He "set my feet on a rock;" here, He is "my crag...my rescuer...my rock in whom I seek refuge." There, "I have come into the watery depths; the flood sweeps me away;" here, "currents of evil terrified me." Where can this come from but the indelible experiences of one who has known the desert in all its seasons and all its guises?

The following words of Isaiah can also be understood only by peering out of the little cleft in the canyon wall through the curtain of falling water. The description is inverted, so that where before it was the aridity that conquered the raging torrent, here the streams of water in the desert satisfy the weary soul:

"Behold, a king shall reign in righteousness, and ministers shall govern with justice. Every one of them shall be like a refuge from gales, a shelter from rainstorms; like brooks of water in arid country, like the shade of a massive rock in an exhausted land." (19)   (Isaiah 32:1-2)

Protection from enemies, from tyrants, from dangers threatening the individual and the nation are portrayed in all the verses cited above through images taken from day-to-day life in the desert: defense from the raging floods on the one hand and from the lack of water and the deadly dryness on the other.

19. "An exhausted land"
As was mentioned earlier, "tired" in Biblical language indicates not only physical exhaustion, but also hunger and thirst. "An exhausted land" describes

Watercourses in the Negev vs. watercourses in the desert

Psalm 126 is one of the most joyful and best-known in Jewish tradition:

> "When the Lord returns the exiles to Zion — we see it as in a dream — our mouths shall be filled with laughter, our tongues, with songs of joy. Then shall they say among the nations: The Lord has done great things for them! The Lord will do great things for us and we shall rejoice. Return our exiles, O Lord, **like watercourses in the Negev**. They who sow in tears shall reap with songs of joy. He goes along weeping, carrying the

the essence of those arid, sunbaked areas that produce fatigue and thirst in any traveler. Such an expression is rooted in actual experience of the tiredness in this burnt-out land.

seed-bag, [but] he shall come back with songs of joy carrying his sheaves." (Psalm 126:1-6)

The description of the return to Israel from exile "like watercourses in the Negev" appears to many as an expression of hope that the returnees shall flood the Land like the torrents of water previously described. But why does the psalmist specify **watercourses in the Negev rather than** simply **in the desert**? And why "watercourses" in the plural rather than "wadi," "stream," or "watercourse"? The answer lies in the difference between the collecting basins in the Negev and those of the wadis in the Judean Desert. The collecting basins of the Negev streams, both those flowing east like Nahal Zin or Nahal Paran and those flowing west like Nahal Shikma, Nahal Gaza, or Nahal El Arish, are incomparably larger than the relatively narrow ones feeding into the wadis of the Judean Desert. When rain falls on the Negev mountains, water begins to flow slowly in many hundreds of tiny rivulets that drain into dozens of larger watercourses. These carry the water in ever-increasing strength to the larger streams that sometimes reach a width of several hundred meters. This picture of **water gathering in small rivulets from distant corners of huge areas and coming together in one broad, deep stream** is surely what inspired the psalmist to pray for the ingathering of the exiles from the four corners of the earth like the "watercourses in the Negev."

Jeremiah alludes to exactly the same broad watercourses in the Negev in a threatening description of what will befall Gaza when the Egyptians will conquer the Philistine stronghold:

> "Thus said the Lord: See, waters are rising from the north. **They shall become a raging torrent, they shall flood the land and all therein, the city and its inhabitants**." (Jeremiah 47:2)

Jeremiah did not exaggerate. Such floods occurred not only in Biblical times; they have also happened in our day. Both Gaza and El-Arish have suffered more than once in the last century from heavy floods that washed away people and property.

But in some years the rain is insufficient to produce even a small flow in the wadis. Such years are a terrible hardship for all who live in the desert:

> "The cattle are exhausted, the herds of oxen distressed because they have no pasture; the flocks of sheep waste away. To Thee I cry, O Lord. The fire has devoured the desert pastures and the flames have burnt up all the trees of the countryside. The very cattle in the field look up to Thee; **for the watercourses are dried up**, and fire has devoured the desert pastures." (Joel 1:18-20)

"The still waters"

After all the descriptions of treacherous waters, dangerous eddies and waterfalls, dry wadis, and empty cisterns, it is much easier to understand the full meaning of the phrase "still waters," or, to be more faithful to the Hebrew text, "restful waters." There is palpable relief at having escaped the storms and floods of the desert into the secure peace of "still waters." When the flood waters in the wadis have disappeared, rivulets of water remain shimmering in the sun, gurgling quietly as they flow slowly along, sometimes disappearing into the bed of the wadi only to reappear among the water-worn rocks and pebbles and on the flat rock tables. This wonderful phrase also encompasses the full water holes and the still water lying in them, which is purified as the silt carried down from the mountains settles slowly to the bottom. In such a setting the words of the psalm truly echo from the clear water: **"The Lord is my shepherd, I shall not want. He maketh me to lie down in green pastures; He leadeth me beside the still [restful] waters."**

The Negev Desert blooms after a heavy rain.

Chapter III

"He restoreth my soul; He leadeth me in the paths of righteousness for His name's sake." (Psalm 23:3)

Confusing Trails in the Desert

Orientation in the desert is not easy. In many areas, the hills look exactly alike, while the many narrow valleys are frequently blocked by rockfalls that further impede the desert traveler. But strangely, no less than the multitude of identical-looking hills and twisting ravines, **the desert trails themselves hamper orientation in this region**. Created by wild animals grazing on the slopes and hills and by the feet of shepherds and their flocks, these trails are scattered the length and breadth of the desert. From each temporary stopping place, paths are trampled to nearby cisterns, or to distant springs, or from the pens to the grazing areas. The flocks, traveling the same route many times, wear out a wide, light-colored path, visible from afar. But in the course of cropping the vegetation on the steep hill slopes, thousands of narrow tracks are formed. These give the sheep and goats the necessary footholds to graze without losing their balance. The distance between one track and the next is the maximum distance a goat can stretch its neck without moving to reach its food.

Of course not only sheep and goats create these tracks. Gazelles and ibex use them as grazing "platforms." They are also used by carnivores to stalk their prey. Because the rains are not strong enough to wash them away, and in these parts of the desert no plows are used that would erase their traces (as happens constantly in the agricultural hill country), these tracks last for years, even after the animals are gone and grazing has stopped. These narrow trails are so typical of all the slopes in Israel's deserts that they inevitably form an integral part of any desert description. Whenever an image of the desert comes to mind, I immediately see the myriad of slender tracks "terracing" the slopes, with the occasional short, diagonal track connecting one level to the next, forming an unforgettable cross-hatched painting.

Yet these grazing tracks, so typical of the desert, are a hazard to the wayfarer. Sometimes the trail traverses a steep slope and

becomes ever narrower until it reaches the edge of an abyss. Above and below it numerous light-colored tracks glimmer, some of them broad and conspicuous, so that the track followed gets lost in the proliferation. Are you still on the right path or have you lost your way without noticing the intersections? Perhaps the hiker with a sense of humor wonders, "How does a goat who fears heights manage?" What is the right decision? To continue along the narrow track at the edge of the abyss or return the way you came and find a more likely continuation of the path? You decide to return. The track you return by merges with its twins to the right and left, and once again you find yourself on the main path you followed, not noticing any junction you should have taken. What now? Should you try to conquer your fear and follow the track back down to the edge of the drop and pretend you are a goat, or continue to backtrack until you find another path

that will perhaps lead you to your destination? You make the decision: continue to backtrack until you find a reasonable trail in the right direction. Finally, after a long search, you find a clearly defined fork that will certainly lead you safely to your goal. Confidently, you change direction and set off. The path takes you slightly further up the slope, then down into the ravine and up the next hill, broadens and...encircles the next hill in exactly the opposite direction of where you want to go! Exhaustion begins to show on your face, your water is running low, and you are on the verge of dropping down and saying, "I'm not going to budge from here. I can't go a step further."

The prophet Jeremiah, a shepherd in the desert along with other youngsters from the town of Anatot, was unquestionably familiar with all the landscapes mentioned throughout this book and faced the challenges of these desert vistas. All these are reflected in the book of Jeremiah much more intimately than in the words of any other prophet, not

1. The parable of the lost sheep

The theme of the lost sheep is also found in the New Testament:

"If one of you has a hundred sheep and loses one of them, does he not leave the ninety-nine in the open pasture and go after the missing one until he has found it? How delighted he is then. He lifts it on his shoulders and carries it home. Then he calls his friends and neighbors together crying: Rejoice with me! I have found my lost sheep. In the same way, I tell you, there will be greater joy in heaven over one sinner who repents than over ninety-nine righteous people who do not need to repent." (Luke 15:4-7 and similarly Matthew 18:12-14)

only in metaphor and simile but also in the style peculiar to Jeremiah. For example, let us return to a verse already quoted:

"My people were lost sheep:[1] their shepherds misled them, the hills led them astray; they roamed from mount to hill, they forgot their own resting place. All who encountered them devoured them; and their foes said: We shall not be held guilty, because they have sinned against the Lord, the true Pasture, the Gathering Place of their fathers — the Lord." (Jeremiah 50:6-7)

This realistic portrayal could be found only in the book of Jeremiah. It summarizes a way of thinking clearly present in most of his descriptions of the nation's sins: **the nation-flock sinned against God because it left Him and wandered off on strange paths to search after foreign gods.**

These verses contain a note of extenuation: the greater part of the blame lies with the shepherds, the leaders of the people. The flock would not have left the good pasture where it had grazed in peace had not the shepherds driven it along the misleading paths of other gods until the flock itself lost its sense of direction. Jeremiah sees Israel as a flock lost in the desert, wandering along paths of different faiths and foreign gods, caught between the ascending and descending power of foreign rulers and armies. The nation-flock roamed from "mount to hill" because it forgot the way back to the secure resting place — to the true God who was the "gathering place of their fathers," the gathering place of the flock, the source of justice, the protected pens where the flock could rest from its wandering and be secure.

This is the basic picture perceived by the prophet: **the people misled on convoluted paths after leaving the "true Pasture."** The misleading was mostly the fault of the shepherds, but the nation — the flock — is also implicated and must share in the punishment: "All who encountered them devoured them" — because by following unknown paths, like the erring goats, they became an easy target of every beast of prey. Therefore their foes say, "We shall not be held guilty"

for slaying them, because they themselves sinned by leaving the safe paths, the "gathering place of their fathers." These enemies shall not be smitten with the evil of which Jeremiah warned: "All who ate of [Israel] were held guilty; disaster befell them." (Jeremiah 2:3)

One more word in chapter 50 verses 6-7 deserves special attention. The usual interpretation is that the shepherds led the people astray by leading them to the hills. But desert experience teaches that **the hills themselves can confuse and lead astray.**(2) And Jeremiah does, in fact, say that **the hills** did something to the people. The word used is *shovevum* שובבום, translated as "led them astray," although "led them in circles" would be more accurate. The infinitive, *lashuv* לשוב, means "to return." In fact, there is a similar

2. The mountains' circle dance

On a Society for the Preservation of Nature in Israel hike in the southern part of the Judean Desert, as we surveyed the primordial scene that spread out from the top of Mount Ittai, the young guide pointed to two mountains, Ribai and Hoddai, rising above the surrounding hills. (Incidentally, Israel's official place-naming authority appropriately named these mountains for two of David's warrior-companions, Ittai and Hoddai, not forgetting Ribbai, Ittai's father! II Samuel 23:29-30) According to the guide, the instructors of the Ein Gedi Field School report that these three

99

element in the English word of "return": to turn and turn again — **re**-turn — circling back to the starting point. The *shovav* שובב, therefore, is one who makes a mistake and repeats it — turns and returns — without knowing how to get out of the maze. Jeremiah describes the people guided by the shepherds along erroneous and futile paths, continuing on their mistaken ways "from mount to hill," while the very hills turn them round and round in endless, misleading circles.

But Jeremiah's attitude toward the *shovevut*, the repeated wrongdoing, of the Kingdom of Israel (which in his day had already been punished by the Assyrian conquest of the Northern Kingdom and the exile of the population) differs greatly from his view of the Kingdom of Judah, which has learned nothing from the experience of its northern sister: "Backsliding Israel has shown herself more in the right than treacherous Judah." (Jeremiah 3:11) The difference is clear — Israel was only

mountains, Ittai, Ribai, and Hoddai, constantly do a circle dance. "From different observation points they appear to be at different angles to eath other, so that we frequently confuse one with the others." This homespun story told by the young guide familiar with desert trails testifies to the accuracy of Jeremiah's expression "the hills led them in circles" — until they realized that "lies echo from the hills, from the multitude of mountains," (Jeremiah 3:23) which seem to dance in circles, changing their position at every turn!

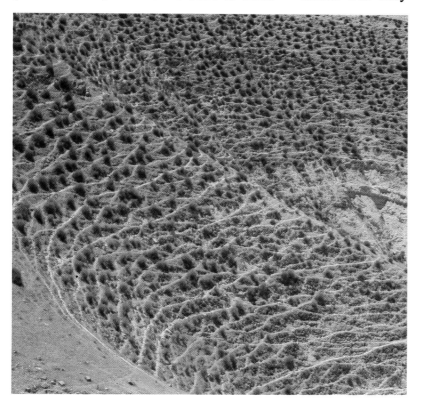

mistaken, while Judah betrayed with malice aforethought:

"Have you seen what backsliding Israel did, going to every high mountain and under every leafy tree, and whoring there? I thought: after she has done all these things, she will return to Me. But she did not return; and her sister, treacherous Judah, saw it. Because backsliding Israel had committed adultery, I cast her off and handed her a bill of divorce; yet her sister, treacherous Judah, was not afraid — she

too went and whored...And after all that, her sister,
treacherous Judah, did not return to Me
wholeheartedly, but insincerely — declares the
Lord." (Jeremiah 3:6-10)

In contrast to misled and mistaken Israel, Jeremiah sees
treacherous Judah as refusing to admit her errors and even
perpetuating them:

"When men fall, do they not get up again? If they
turn away, do they not repent and return *(yashuv
v'lo yashuv]* ? Why is this people – Jerusalem –
turned away *[shoveva]* with a perpetual turning
away *[meshova]* [from Me]? They cling to deceit,
they refuse to return *[lashuv]*. I have listened and
heard: they do not speak honestly. No one repents

his wickedness saying: What have I done!
Everyone turns to his wayward course, like a steed
dashing forward into battle." (Jeremiah 8:4-6)

Jeremiah uses the root *shuv* שוב with double meaning, as a
word game. If they return *(yashuv)* from their backsliding,
will they not repent *(yashuv)* of their errant waywardness?
Yet, cries the prophet, the people of Jerusalem turned away
(shovevu) with a persistent, perpetual turning away
(mosheva), refusing to return from their treacherous ways,
and still they continue to refuse to return *(lashuv)*. The word
lashuv לשוב appears many times in Jeremiah, while other
prophets use the term most sparingly (twice in Hosea, once in

Isaiah, and once in Micah). This word is an inseparable part of Jeremiah's inimitable style, imbued with the desert in all its aspects. But Jeremiah does not stop with this castigation. To express the full measure of his bitterness at the perpetually devious ways of the Kingdom of Judah, Jeremiah continues with an image from the animal world of the Judean Desert, where he observed the flocks of birds in their seasonal migrations:

"Even the stork in the sky knows her seasons, and the turtledove, swift, and crane keep the time of their coming."   (Jeremiah 8:7)

Uzi Paz, one of Israel's leading ornithologists, writes about the migrations of the storks: "During the fall migration, there are almost no migrating storks seen in the west of Israel. Most of them pass to the east of the Jordan River, as well as along the Syrian-African Rift. They are seen primarily in the Bet Shean Valley, along the shores of the Dead Sea, occasionally in the Arava Valley and the wadis emptying into it, and in the area of Eilat. In spring, the main migratory routes pass to the north of the Gulf of Suez, spreading over the northern Sinai and western Negev deserts, moving over the Jordan Valley via the Beersheba Depression, converging through the Bet Shean Valley. The hot easterly winds which prevail during this migratory season blow many storks off course, forcing them to the coastal plain. Then their migration is slower and it is possible to see them all over Israel: in pasturelands, in fields, near puddles of water and in fish ponds, and even in the desert." (*The Nature Encyclopaedia of Eretz Yisrael*, Ministry of Defense, 1986, vol. 6, pp. 77-78.)

As opposed to the turtledove, swift, and crane mentioned by Jeremiah, **the stork is unique in the variance of its migratory paths in the spring and fall.** While the inhabitants of the region west of the mountains were used to seeing only the spring migration of the stork, Jeremiah was able to observe the flocks of storks migrating south in autumn over the Judean Desert and the Dead Sea. That is why he says the stork "knows her seasons" (plural) while the turtledove, swift, and crane "keep the time (singular) of their coming." Furthermore, Jeremiah saw the stork winging its way in the sky year after year, season after season, without turning off the right "paths," as the sharpest contrast to the people of Jerusalem, who kept the ways of foreign gods and did not even repent betraying the true God.

Pain at the people's misdirection and their persistent use of wrong roads occurs in another of Jeremiah's prophecies, remarkable for its forgiving tone. Although neither the shepherds nor the flock are mentioned, in light of all that was explained above the metaphor is nevertheless clear, including its parallel to the image of the lost flock in verses 6-7 of chapter 50 (p.98).

Flocks of cranes in the Sharon Valley

"Hark! on the bare heights (*shfayim* שפיים) [3] is heard the suppliant weeping of the people of Israel, for they have gone a crooked way, forgetting the Lord their God. **Return, backsliding children**, I will heal your futile circling! Here we are, we come to You, for You, O Lord, are our God! Surely, **lies echo from the hills, from the multitude of mountains**. Only through the Lord our God is there deliverance for Israel. But idol worship has consumed the crops of our fathers ever since our youth." (Jeremiah 3:21-24)

The prophet hears the lamentation and wailing rising from "the bare heights." What are these voices of "suppliant weeping" that shake his soul? And whom are they addressing? These are the voices of **the lost sheep**, the Children of Israel who "have gone a crooked way," becoming lost on false paths that literally misled them among the desert hills, forgetting their enclosures, their true pastures, and unable to find their way back. But at the moment they admit the error of their ways and begin contritely to search for the way back, the prophet hears the call of God to them: **"Return, O backsliding children"** – return, you who took wrong paths; "I will heal your futile circling," because I know the true path and it is in My power to "heal" your delusion. This confident and strong voice is heard from afar and signals the way to the lost pasture, to the safe sheepfold whose location they forgot. And they immediately stop their bitter weeping, shake off the despair of those lost in the desert, and joyfully answer: **"Here we are, we come to You."** They come towards Him and admit their sin, relieved to be free of the hills and "the multitude of mountains" that gave the illusion of being vantage points from which they could find the right road. Finally, the "backsliding children" realize that these endless hills and mountains in the desert are but deluding promises leading to perdition. Indeed the endless bare heights, so similar in appearance, are one of the main reasons travelers lose their way in the desert. Jeremiah refers to them many times when he speaks of the reasons the nation came to such grief.

Migrating storks in the Judean Desert

3. What are the *shfayim*?

The word *shfayim* שפיים appears eight times in the Bible: twice in Isaiah and six times in Jeremiah. The contexts clearly indicates that the reference is to the same desert hills described in this chapter. English translators agree that "bare hills" reasonably conveys the sense of the Hebrew word. Because these hills are composed of soft chalk, they have a singular shape: steep flanks and sharp or rounded tops that from a distance appear to have been smoothed and polished over centuries, as if shaped by a majestic sculptor. It seems that this special appearance gave them the Hebrew name *shfayim* שפיים, from the root *shuf* שוף, to smooth or polish.

The traveler sitting on a moonlit night on a mountain top facing the white desert hills, the endless gleaming slopes, and the moon-tinted waters of the Dead Sea, with fine mists covering and uncovering the mountain barrier on the eastern horizon, occasionally hearing the song of the lonely shepherd in the enchanted desert night, answered from somewhere by the distant, lone fox whose voice evokes a chorus of prolonged howls — only one who sees and hears all this can feel the full force of the verses of the prophet from Anatot.

I by no means intend to imply that Jeremiah literally deals with getting lost in the desert. This is only the poetic image for the idol worship and cult practices that were carried out "on every high hill" (Jeremiah 2:20). This is the constant picture in Jeremiah's mind when he speaks of Israel's sins and her straying from the path of God.

It is illuminating to underscore the parallels in the two passages discussed above, Jeremiah 3:21-24 and 50:6-7:

From Chapter 3	*From Chapter 50*
the people of Israel have gone a crooked way	their *shepherds* misled them
they have *gone a crooked way*	they *roamed from mount to hill*
forgetting *the Lord their God*	forgot their own *resting place*
God is *deliverance* and *safety*	*God* is the *true Pasture*, the *gathering place* of their fathers
idol worship has *consumed* the crops of the people	all who encountered them *devoured* them

At the crossroads

The same desert-imbued shepherding experiences suffuse Jeremiah's words in the following:

"Cry out in joy for Jacob. Shout at the crossroads of the nations! Sing aloud in praise, and say: Save,

O Lord, Your people, the remnant of Israel. I will bring them in from the northland, gather them from the ends of the earth — the blind and the lame among them, those with child and those in labor. In a vast throng they shall return here. They shall come with weeping, and with supplication will I guide them. I will lead them to streams of water, (4) by a level road where they will not stumble. For I am ever a Father to Israel..."   (Jeremiah 31:6-8)

Seemingly there is a contradiction here: at first the prophet

Comparison to Isaiah 49:9-10
These verses from Jeremiah are reminiscent of the description in Isaiah (mentioned in chapter I, pp. 37-38):
"They shall pasture along the roads, on every bare hill shall be their pasture. They shall not hunger or thirst; hot wind and sun shall not strike them; for He who loves them will lead them, He will guide them to springs of water." These words, too, express a sense of relief, but there is neither weeping nor supplication.

Desert flood following a heavy rainfall in the Negev mountains

describes **joy and shouting** when Israel hears of its return from exile – and suddenly Jeremiah says that this redemption shall be with **weeping and supplication**! What do these have to do with shouts of joy?

The Jewish commentators such as Rashi and Radak understood this weeping as tears of joy. But indeed, why weeping and why the need for supplication? Has there ever been an expression of joy through supplication? And who is doing the supplicating? Is it the nation begging God for its salvation? Why, when they have already been forgiven and God is leading them back to their land with joy, and there is nothing more to be gained by this supplication?

Indeed, no other prophet combines tears and supplication with the joy of the return to Israel. On the contrary, Isaiah calls out in his prophecy of comfort: "Yea, you shall leave [Babylon] in **joy and** be led home in **peace**. Before you, mount and hill shall shout aloud, and all the trees of the field shall **clap** their **hands**." (Isaiah 55:12) Such descriptions of happiness appear in several places in Isaiah.

It seems to me that the weeping and entreaty can be understood only by considering Jeremiah's mental picture when he imagined the return of the Children of Israel to their land and their God. This is the image of the lost sheep, of the people misled in the desert, whose voice is heard on the bare hills seeking the right road: "on the bare heights is heard the suppliant weeping of the people of Israel." (Jeremiah 3:21) This is the weeping and the entreaty, and it is this very weeping and supplication that moves God to save them. He shows them the right path by which to return to Him and to His land; after they fall time and again on winding roads and become tired to death of thirst and hunger, He leads them with joy and shouts of rejoicing "to streams of water by a level road where they will not stumble." (Jeremiah 31:8) This is the metaphor embedded in Jeremiah's soul and woven into his prophecy: the return to the Land of Israel and true faith led by the God of Israel, Who appeared in the moment of weeping and entreaty by those who had lost their way.

The very same picture is found in chapter 50, in Jeremiah's

description of the return to Zion:

> "In those days and at that time, declares the Lord, the people of Israel together with the people of Judah shall come, and they shall weep as they go to seek the Lord their God. They shall inquire for Zion; in that direction their faces shall turn; they shall come and attach themselves to the Lord by a covenant for all time, which shall never be forgotten."
> (Jeremiah 50:4-5)

This vision of the future return to Zion was quite intentionally joined to verses 6-7, "My people were lost sheep..." (discussed on p. 98), which allude to cleansing the nation's sin by laying blame for their straying on the shepherds who **mis**led them. The nation's leaders'-shepherds' guilt confronts them in another prophecy by Jeremiah that was discussed in chapter I (p. 38):

> "Oh **shepherds who let the flock of My pasture stray and scatter!** — declares the Lord. Assuredly, thus said the Lord, the God of Israel, concerning the shepherds who should tend My people: **It is you who let My flock scatter and go astray.** You did not count them, but I am going to have you account for your wicked acts — declares the Lord. And I myself will gather the remnant of My flock from all the lands to which I have banished them, and I will bring them back to their pasture, where they shall be fertile and increase. And I will appoint over them shepherds who will tend them; they shall not longer fear or be dismayed, and none of them shall be missing — declares the Lord."
> (Jeremiah 23:1-4)

The search for the right path is the motif of still other prophecies of Jeremiah, prophecies that express the same central idea: **straying from God is like leaving the tranquil and safe sheepfold for the deception of misleading paths of foreign gods and idol worship; the return to God is like deliverance from this deception and finding the road back to the central**

sheepfold, "the gathering place of their fathers."

"Thus said the Lord: Stop at the crossroads and consider. Inquire about the paths of the world: which is the good road? Travel it, and **find tranquillity** for yourselves. But they said: We will not go."   (Jeremiah 6:16)

Truly, standing at the crossroads and puzzling over which fork leads to "the good road" is a choice that constantly faces the desert wayfarer. Even Jeremiah — or perhaps especially Jeremiah — could have been preoccupied when walking with his flock, sunk in thoughts of what he would say to the people of Jerusalem. With his mind abstracted, could he not have found himself at a crossroads, wondering which was the right path to the gathering place of the sheep? The description "and find **tranquillity** for yourselves" dramatizes that this experience struck a deep chord in Jeremiah. The "tranquillity" conveys the intense relief when the traveler discovers that he has indeed chosen the fork that leads him to his destination. Jeremiah hears God calling to His people to cease going blindly down twisting paths, to stop and choose the right way among all the different paths. But they do not obey His words. They stiffen their necks and say, "We will not go." **"This people has a wayward and defiant heart; they have turned aside and gone their way."** (Jeremiah 5:23) Stubbornly and impudently they left the good road for the paths of evil. In verse 14:10, again the same image: **"Truly they love to stray, they have not restrained their feet."** With pleasure they travel along the wrong paths and do not stop their feet from treading on corrupting roads.

The phrase "they have not restrained their feet" could only have occurred to Jeremiah through his own experience of the extensive walking required in the desert, especially when it is crucial to reach one's destination before nightfall. Then one must keep walking, ignoring fatigue and sore, swollen feet. This expression is reminiscent of Moses' reminder of the wonders that occurred during the wandering in the desert: "The clothes upon you did not wear out, **nor did your feet swell these forty years."** (Deuteronomy 8:4)

The image of losing one's way and the **relief** when the right road is found appears also in the following verses:

5. "From afar the Lord appeared to me."

On one level, these words pertain to the exiles of the Kingdom of Israel, far from the Land of Israel: God appears to come from afar to comfort and save them. But the source of the expression "from afar" can only be understood by one who has often experienced the secret wonders of the desert.

In the Judean Desert and the Negev hills are areas strewn with flint rocks, bare of almost all vegetation and broken by undulating low, wide, long hills that

"A people that survived the sword found favor **in the desert; [I will] go to comfort him — Israel. From afar the Lord appeared to me**.[5] Eternal love I conceived for you then, therefore I continue my unfailing care for you."

(Jeremiah 31:1-2)

As in the exchange in chapter 3 (verse 22) — God calls His backsliding children to return and the sinful nation penitently replying, "Here we are, we come to You," — here, too, the "people that survived the sword" wandering in the desert search for the way back to "the true Pasture" and **suddenly discover God from afar** coming towards them to **comfort** them and show them the way. Especially poignant here is the cry of the people who have transgressed in the desert where **"from afar** the Lord appeared to them," followed by God's immediate response, **"Eternal love I conceive for you, therefore I continue my unfailing care for you"** (in the sense that true love forgives all, as in Proverbs 10:12: **"Love covers up all faults."**)

Until now the sources of inspiration have been the vistas and perils of the desert. Jeremiah continues with the prophecies of comfort (quoted in chapter I, p. 25) that describe the rebuilding of the destroyed Kingdom of Israel and its return to the national and spiritual center of Jerusalem:

block out even a glimpse of the horizon. Sometimes the hiker finds himself on steep slopes that obstruct everything but the next turn in a dry stream bed. But as the wayfarer continues around the top curve of the hill, or breaks out of the confining walls of the canyon, or comes to the edge of the flint-strewn wasteland, he is overwhelmed by a breathtaking view. His startled eye takes in the panorama and then picks up both the close and distant details:

Here are several angular, whitish-yellow hills playing hide and seek with each other, and another chain of flanks further away, and then a plain, and still further away a change to a bluish color, the first glimpse of the Dead Sea. Still further east a mountain wall draws the eye from north to south for a distance of many dozens of kilometers, until the barrier grows faint in the mists of the far south, somewhere in the mountains of Edom, near Mount Seir.

I believe this unique utterance, "from afar the Lord appeared to me," came to Jeremiah through the inspiration of stirring vistas he saw on his desert sojourns. Perhaps only the traveler who reaches such unexpected overlooks can understand the overwhelming sense of presence the view evokes. Jeremiah may have also been inspired by much earlier words spoken by Moses:

"The Lord came from Sinai; He shone upon them from Seir..."

(Deuteronomy 33:2)

Here Jeremiah sharpens his vision and sees from afar the edges of Seir enveloped in the distant mists; there God "shone" in Moses's blessing of the Children of Israel. For Jeremiah, "from afar" means "from the other side of the Land of Israel," far from where "the Lord appeared to me."

"I will build you up again, O maiden Israel, and you shall be rebuilt. Again you shall take up your timbrels and go forth to the rhythm of the dancers. Again you shall plant vineyards on the hills of Samaria. Men shall plant and live to enjoy them. For the day is coming when watchmen shall proclaim on the heights of Ephraim: Come, let us go up to Zion, to the Lord our God!" (Jeremiah 31:4-6)

The misleading paths in the desert find expression also in the following passage:

"For My people have forgotten Me. They sacrifice to delusion. The paths of the world made them stumble onto byways, on a road not paved."

(Jeremiah 18:15)

Most commentators, translators, and scholars have had difficulty understanding this verse. A literal reading indicates that "the paths of the world" are those that misled the Children of Israel. It was not understood how paths clearly intended for walking were the very ones that misled the people. Also puzzling was the concentration of different names for "road." Not only Biblical critics but also the traditional commentators struggled with this verse. Radak, for instance, claims that the word "to leave" is missing before "paths of the world" and that it was omitted because it was self-evident. Accordingly, he suggests reading the verse: "They stumble in their ways to leave the paths of the world." Biblical critics delved primarily into stylistic problems and the structure of the verse, without success. The supplementary examples of their tortuous efforts show what can befall serious scholars when they lack knowledge of the soil whence the words they are criticizing have sprung.[6]

To those familiar with Israel's deserts, this verse presents no problem. The reader already knows that one of the hazards for the desert traveler is precisely those tracks, paths, trails, and roads that branch off and multiply, then come together and branch off again. This is what Jeremiah is saying: **The ways of the world are the perverse ways of the strangers and their foreign gods, who enticed the people and**

lured them away to serve other gods; the paths thus diverted the people from the straight way and caused them to walk on byways instead of a paved (smooth) road.

The problems of orientation in the desert also find expression in the following:

> "Thus said the Lord: What wrong did your fathers find in Me that they abandoned Me and went after delusion and were deluded? They never asked themselves: Where is the Lord Who brought us up from the land of Egypt, Who led us through the desert, a land of wilderness and canyons, an arid land, a land of the shadow of death, a land no man had traversed, where no human being had dwelt? "And I brought you to this fruitful land to enjoy its fruit and its bounty..." (Jeremiah 2:5-7)

The prophet is astonished that the nation that has sinned and lost its way still does not acknowledge the God Who led it to its goal through the desert and its obstacles. The consequences are self-evident:

6. Higher Biblical criticism

This is not the place to describe the impact of 19th century German Biblical scholarship on modern Bible study, but a few examples of the effort to "correct" the text of Jeremiah 18:15 may be of interest. The original Hebrew text is:

"כי שכחני עמי, לשוא יקטרו, ויכשלום בדרכיהם שבילי עולם ללכת נתיבות דרך לא סלולה."

Ki shekhekhuni ami, lashav yekateru, vayekhshilum b'darkhehem sh'vilei olam lalekhet netivot derekh lo s'lula.

D. Rotstein in *Das Buch Jeremiah* (Kautzsch, Die Heiligen Schriften des Alten Testaments, 1922), offers this footnote to the phrase beginning with *lalekhet netivot*: "From the rhythmic aspect it would be possible to suffer this colorless phrase, but it is more accurate to see it as an extraneous glossary of terms which serves no purpose."

D. T. Voltz, in *Studien zum Text des Jeremiah* (1920), decided that the entire second half of verse 15 has no meaning. Why should there be four different words signifying "road"? Obviously, there are too many and these ruin the dirge quality of the verse. "I am convinced that *shvilei olam* is not in the correct place and should be moved to follow the word *ami*, unlike Duhm [another 19th-century German Bible critic] who would remove it entirely. I believe that the word *derekh* should be removed altogether because it was obviously added merely to explain *lo s'lula*."

Other scholars have insisted that the Masoretic text was in error for various reasons: Jeremiah's rhythmic scheme was upset by the last nine words of the verse, which therefore belonged, in various combinations, to either the previous or the following verses; also suggested were changes in word order, substitution of new words, or removal altogether of words that did not suit the patterns presumed to be authentic.

"Lions have roared and growled at him, have made his land a waste. His cities are razed to the ground and abandoned...**Is it not your desertion of the Lord your God while He was leading you on the road that brings all this upon you?**" (Jeremiah 2:15-16)

The God of Israel is the people's steadfast shepherd, Who led them in the great desert stretching from Egypt to the land of Edom, through countries following strange gods, surviving wars and other adversities "by a level road where they will not stumble" (Jeremiah 31:8). Yet this people (and its leaders) did

not sufficiently value the Leader of the flock, Who alone knew the right paths; they stopped following Him and took to other, foreign ways. The result: the people became hopelessly lost and were overwhelmed by strangers. In the succeeding verses, Jeremiah explains his words, criticizing the loss of political direction and describing the evils wrought by the policy of playing off the superpowers of Assyria and Egypt against each other:

> "What, then, is the good of your going to Egypt to drink the waters of the Nile? And what is the good of your going to Assyria to drink the waters of the Euphrates? Let your evil reprove you, let your backsliding rebuke you; **mark well how bad and bitter it is that you forsake the Lord your God.**"
> (Jeremiah 2:18-19)

In other words, their mistakes along the way were the result of backsliding and will cause the people to suffer. Now they will pay the bitter price for leaving the Lord, Who was there to lead them on the right way.

After all that has been said concerning the misleading paths in the desert, it will not be difficult to understand the singular idea expressed by Jeremiah and not any other prophet:

> "**Erect markers, set up signposts**; keep in mind the track, the road that you traveled."
> (Jeremiah 31:20)

This verse could serve as the motto of Israel's National Committee for Trail Marking. In fact, in recent years, young people directed by the Society for the Protection of Nature in Israel field schools have done much work marking trails in the desert. These projects perpetuate the ancient tradition of erecting markers in the desert. Signposts were even more vital for earlier generations without detailed topographical maps, compasses, or two-way radios to summon help. Here and there in the Judean, Negev, and Sinai deserts, one can still see small stone cairns built up by trailsides. These served as markers for the trade caravans that have crossed the desert since the dawn of history.

left and upper right: *Rock markers painted by the Society for the Protection of Nature in Israel indicate hiking trails in the Judean Desert.* **bottom right**: *Stone cairn in the desert*

Without the painted marker, few hikers could figure out how to get down the 300 m cliff from the Bokek Ascent in the Judean Desert to the Dead Sea.

The above verse from Jeremiah continues:

> "Return, maiden Israel! Return to these towns of yours! How long will you waver, O backsliding daughter *(bat shoveva* בת שובבה)." (Jeremiah 31:20-21)

Once again Jeremiah uses the term *shovav/shoveva* in the sense of taking the wrong road. Only this meaning can logically connect these words and the previous verse. The time has come for the backsliding daughter to find her way and return to her God and her city.

In light of all that has been discussed heretofore, we can conclude this chapter with the words that began it:

> "He **restoreth** *(yeshovev)* my soul; He leadeth me in the **paths of righteousness** for His name's sake." (Psalms 23:3)

Again, *yeshovev* ישובב is used in the sense of **re**-turning the soul, bringing it back, **re**-storing it. The translation "**paths** of righteousness" fails to give the unique sense of the Hebrew words, *ma'aglei tzedek,* מעגלי צדק, meaning "**circles** of righteousness." With this definition, the poetic image emerges of God leading the shepherd in **circles of righteousness** and not in the **misleading circles** by which the hills entrapped the unwary wayfarer.

These few words of the psalm encapsulate all the desert vistas described in this chapter and all the innermost thoughts these landscapes evoked in our forefathers. The many desert tracks spring at us from this verse: the tracks that encircle the bare mountain hills, and those that in good years lead to green pastures. The sinning and backsliding soul, misled by the hills that drove it in circles, was healed by Him Who called for His renegade children to return. This is the same soul that stood at the crossroads seeking the way to repose, finding it when the Shepherd redirected Israel along the right path "to its oasis." (Jeremiah 50:19) The same paths that misled the soul to follow roads not smoothed over could lead it, under the direction of the good and forgiving Shepherd, to the paths of righteousness. These, in turn, lead to the true pasture, the gathering place of the fathers, intimated in the words "for His name's sake."

Chapter IV:

"Yea, though I walk through the valley of the shadow of death, I will fear no evil, for Thou art with me. Thy rod and Thy staff, they comfort me."

(Psalm 23:4)

Terrifying cliffs and canyons

"Where is the Lord...Who led us through the desert, a land of wilderness and canyons...?"   (Jeremiah 2:6)

This chapter will open a window onto the most overpowering vistas of the desert, hidden in its crevasses, invisible from a distance. These spectacular sights — which compellingly lure hikers and boast the most exciting and challenging trails — are found in the wadis that cut into the landscape to the east and west of the Jericho Valley, the Dead Sea, and the Rift Valley between the Dead Sea and Eilat. Geological convulsions, the sinking and rising of soft and hard sediment layers, and the effect of sudden floods have joined to sculpt scenes that always mesmerize even the most experienced hikers. The wonder that these chasms inspire has always made me imagine what our forefathers felt there. What did young David feel when he first came with "those few sheep in the desert" (I Samuel 17:28) to the cliff edge at the narrow entrance to Nahal Og; how did the child Amos respond when he suddenly found himself overlooking the fabulous canyon in the Tekoa Desert among the cliffs of Nahal Kidron? Empathetic with them, standing in the very same places, awestruck by the same scenery, I see how these landscapes are reflected in the words bequeathed to us in the Bible.

An arid land, a land of the shadow of death

Again the first Biblical figure to come to mind is Jeremiah. The prophet from Anatot accompanies us as we walk among the barren desert hills in a broad, sunlit streambed. Under our feet we feel the crunch of dry gravel pulverized by the grinding action of centuries of floodwaters. The reflected glare of the bare, white slopes is blinding in the noon sun, and our pupils contract to minimize the intensity of light. Suddenly we stop in our tracks just at the edge of a yawning abyss, which appears at first glance to be absolutely black in contrast to the surrounding dazzling light. Slowly, while peering into this dark chasm, our pupils dilate and we take in the walls of the abyss dropping one, two, and even three or four hundred meters down. It is impossible to avoid the frightening thought:

What would have happened had we taken another step forward...and in such a moment the words of Jeremiah beg to be read from the Bible:

"Thus said the Lord: What wrong did your fathers find in Me that they abandoned Me and went after delusion and were deluded? They never asked themselves: Where is the Lord, Who brought us up from the land of Egypt, Who led us through the desert, a land of wilderness and canyons, an arid land, a land of the shadow of death, a land no man had traversed, where no human being had dwelt?'"

(Jeremiah 2:5-6)

Looking down at the literal **shadow of death** in the canyon's abyss, after the long hike through the dry riverbed, it is needless to explain "the **arid land, a land of the shadow of death.**" And it is just as unnecessary to ponder the meaning of the words in the twenty-third psalm, **"Yea, though I walk through the valley of the shadow of death, I will fear no evil, for Thou art with me."**

A *land of darkness*

The bright skies and desert sunlight above, coupled with the glare of the desert slopes and the light-colored ground below, fill the entire area with such blazing light that it is difficult to endure. The desert is a land suffused with light from all sides, with too much light, not only for the casual desert wayfarer who comes from the green mountains but also for those who live there. So it seems strange to read in Jeremiah:

> "O generation, behold the word of the Lord: have I been **like a desert** to Israel, **like a land of darkness**? Then why do My people say: We have broken loose, we will not come to You anymore?"
>
> (Jeremiah 2:31)

A land of darkness is clearly **a synonym** here for **the desert**. What is darkness doing in a land whose most striking characteristic is its blinding light? Although none of the traditional commentators such as Rashi or Radak raised this question, some of the translators — followed by the Biblical critics — "resolved" the problem by manipulating the word *ma'pelia* מאפליה (darkness) to read *mapala* מפלה (defeat). But to those familiar with the desert and the emotions it inspires, there is no need for such "clarifications."

The darkness that rapidly blankets the desert at sunset produces the strongest possible contrast to the dazzling light of day. Travelers who are foolhardy enough to walk on in the dark, believing that the bright starlight of the desert is sufficient to light the way, may find themselves falling into "the valley of the shadow of death," or rolling down one of the escarpments invisible in the dark. Both light and darkness are intensified in the desert — and the contrast between them is

133

therefore much sharper than in less light-intense regions. Only short periods at dawn and dusk provide a transition between absolute darkness and absolute light. And it is during these precious moments that the desert reveals its amazing range of color. In the morning, just after sunrise, the soft scene will fade away to be replaced by the overwhelming blaze of sunlight. The process is reversed at evening, when the hidden palette of colors found only in the desert is revealed for the briefest interval before being wrapped in the descending darkness, secreting the paths and tracks that but a few minutes earlier were so easily discernible.

This is the way images of the desert appear to a person who has spent nights and days there: its light and darkness seem to battle each other. This sensation helps clarify Jeremiah's words: Why did the Children of Israel lose their direction? Was God like the desert of searing light and heat, so difficult to bear, or was He perhaps like the cursed darkness of night and of the valleys of the shadow of death? This comparison of God to the desert is not found in the writings of any other prophet. At first glance, the comparison itself is strange. But Jeremiah's intimate association with the desert, the assumption that he felt God's presence in the desert on many occasions, as well as his pondering the 40-year wandering of the Children of Israel in the desert, all elucidate his train of thought and the development of his ideas.

The impressions of the desert's darkness appear in yet other places in Jeremiah:

> "Give honor to the Lord your God before the darkness falls, before your feet stumble on the mountains of evening; when you hope for light and it is turned to the shadow of death, and becomes [pitch] dark." (Jeremiah 13:16)

Here, too, is a description of what typically befalls the desert traveler. As mentioned, the change from light to darkness is very swift and sharp in the desert. It is especially apparent to anyone walking westward in the Judean Desert in late afternoon. While the hills to the east still faintly reflect the last rays of twilight, the slopes to the west are already cast in heavy shadow, warning the traveler that in another few minutes he will have to climb them in utter darkness, while his tired feet stumble on pieces of sharp flint. But even worse than tripping over one's feet on the "mountains of evening" is the disaster the prophet wishes upon those who betray their roles:

> "Prophet and priest alike are godless; even in My House I found their wickedness, declares the Lord. Therefore their path shall become like slippery ground in darkness. They shall skid and fall there for I will bring disaster upon them." (Jeremiah 23:11-12)

The desert darkness is infinitely worse when clouds cover the stars, and the blackness is so intense that the only way to maneuver is to grope with one's hands. Then it is easy to understand the expression "a darkness that can be touched" (Exodus 10:21), describing the ninth plague of Egypt. But

The author with a group of intrepid hikers in the Judean Desert

sometimes these clouds not only mask the starlight, they also release drops of light rain that wet only the surface layer of the desert soil, while the lower layer remains dry and hard. Some 45 years ago I had an experience that made every sinew of my body aware of Jeremiah's curse. I still remember every detail:

It was a dark, cloudy night, and we — a regular group of desert hikers — were on the desert heights between the Dead Sea and Jerusalem, on our way to the place we had selected on the map for our night's camp. Most of the group were already very tired from the walk that had lasted all day and half the night without pause. Every once in a while I would leave the rest of the group and go off with one of the better hikers to scout in the dark for the easiest path by which to continue. While we were some distance away from the rest of the group, who had stayed on the top of the hill, a brief downpour fell on us just as we found a wide and comfortable path. We happily started to return to the waiting company, when within a few moments the entire surface layer of soil became wet and so slippery that we were barely able to continue. When we got to the foot of the hill on which our friends were resting we simply could not climb up. We tried to clamber up by every stratagem, but the slick surface thwarted all our efforts. Luckily, the rain continued to fall, and the underlying soil began to absorb the water; then we were able to cling to the mud and scoop out toeholds and handholds. Only then did we succeed, on all fours, in slowly crawling up the hill, where we collapsed at the feet of our anxious friends.

Cliff and fortress

The curse of slippery darkness is not the only one Jeremiah conjures out of the desert's special circumstances and sights. Another of his curses returns us to the tall cliff walls of the "land of canyons" with whose description this chapter began:

> "Here I am to deal with you, O mountain of the destroyer, declares the Lord, destroyer of the whole earth! I will stretch out My hand against you and roll you down from the crags and make you a burning mountain." (Jeremiah 51:25)

Standing above the terrifying canyon walls that reach heights

of hundreds of meters, and seeing the huge boulders that had rolled down from the crags into the abyss, it is easy to understand the words of the prophet concerning Babylon, Israel's greatest enemy in his day, even though we know — as did Jeremiah — that Babylon was built on flat land without cliffs from which to be toppled.[1] This expression — "**roll you down from the crags**" — is a most natural imprecation in these areas of the desert, uttered by Jeremiah without any intended reference to the specific topography of Babylon. The phrase "**make you a burning mountain**" can be understood if we are aware that not far from the Judean Desert, south of the Dead Sea, stands Mount Sodom, which has symbolized destruction by fire and brimstone since the days of Abraham.

In the prophecies of the destruction of Moab, Jeremiah speaks of these same crags:

> "Abandon the cities and dwell in the crags, O inhabitants of Moab! Be like a dove that nests in the mouth of an abyss."
> (Jeremiah 48:28)

This verse reflects two facts: one — doves nest in the clefts of rocks overlooking the chasms; and two — populations flee from settlements in time of war to the safety of the same rock clefts, which are extremely difficult for the enemy to penetrate. Because of the numerous crevasses and clefts in the Desert of Benjamin, close to the borderline desert settlements, this scene repeated itself many times. It is not surprising that such an image would imbed itself in Jeremiah's mind. Some 400 years earlier, in the days of the Judges, 600 men, the surviving remnant of the tribe of Benjamin, escaped the pursuit of the other tribes of Israel and "fled to the desert, to the **Rock of Rimmon**," where they remained for "four months." (Judges 20:47) In this area, in a wadi near a village today called "Rimmon" in Arabic, there are numerous cliffs punctuated with caves and crevasses in which hundreds of people can find shelter and fortification. From here they can make forays for food to the fields of grain of the borderline desert settlements and to the flocks grazing in the desert, with no one to rout them out of their secure retreats. Here they can be like doves spreading over freshly-sown fields to the west of the desert and at

1. Towers or crags?

Many commentators were astonished by Jeremiah's use of this term, and decided the "crag" in fact was "a symbol of the tall towers of Babylon" (e.g., Radak and Altschuler [*]). Nor did the Biblical critics understand the connection between Babylon and crags; they went so far as to totally invalidate Jeremiah's words: "As to the crags from which one can roll down, there is nothing to discuss." (D. Rotstein, in *Das Buch Jeremiah*)

[*] **Altschuler, David** — 18th century Biblical exegete from Galicia whose lastingly popular and respected commentary on the Prophets and the Writings (Hagiographa) was published in two volumes: *Metzudat Zion* ("Fortress of Zion"), which explains individual words, and *Metzudat David* ("Fortress of David"), which elucidates the meaning of the text.

evening return east to shelter in the clefts of the rocks in the desert's wadis.[2] There is no access to these caverns from above — from the top of the cliffs — nor from the wadis below except on the narrowest of tracks, steep and serpentine, which can be easily guarded by the occupants from inside the caves.

In the days of Saul, before Jonathan's brilliant attack against the Philistines, "the people hid themselves in caves and holes and among the rocks, in pits and cisterns" (I Samuel 13:6) for fear of the mighty Philistine forces. Jeremiah, who was certainly familiar with these historical events and well acquainted with the locations of the caves near his village, while expressing a certain sarcastic commiseration with the fate of the Moabites in his own prophetic fury against them, offers them practical, perhaps mocking advice: **"Abandon the cities...and dwell in the crags."**

In his prophecies against Edom, Jeremiah bears in mind the security that Edom had always found in its famous rocks, and he knows well that they who dwell there can truly rely on these natural fortifications.[3] And yet he announces the certain end prescribed by God:

> "You who dwell in clefts of the rock, who occupy the height of the hill! Though you build your nest high as a vulture, [4] from there I will pull you down, declares the Lord. And Edom shall be desolate; whoever passes by will be appalled...It shall be like the overthrow of Sodom and Gomorrah and their neighbors...No man shall live there, no human shall sojourn there." (Jeremiah 49:16-18)

It is interesting to compare the metaphors used by Jeremiah: he calls on **Moab** to flee to the crags, to "become like a **dove** which nests in the rock-face at the mouth of an abyss," because the dove cannot defend itself, it **can only hide**. On the other hand, he sees **Edom** as the huge, strong **vulture** which lives in the clefts of the rock and is confident not only because of his inaccessible nest but also because of his **enormous strength**. The vulture nesting in the highest crags is also found in the book of Job:

2. Twice a day they cross the desert
"The rock dove is a social bird both during the mating season and the rest of the year. It lives in craggy areas, in narrow canyons and chasms. This is where it nests and hatches its young, while its food is found in the open fields. It also needs drinking water. In the Judean Desert it is possible to track rock doves flying in flocks each morning from the canyon cliffs in the east, westward across the entire width of the desert — some 20 km — and spreading out to feed in the sown fields. Towards noon, they return to drink from the water holes and to shelter in the shade of the rock clefts. In the afternoon they again fly to the fields and at sunset gather in large flocks for the return to their roosts." (Uzi Paz, "Birds," in *Nature Encyclopaedia of Eretz Yisrael*, p. 265)

3. The capture of the rock
It is known that the inhabitants of Edom made excellent use of the natural rock formations of their land. The most famous city in the mountains of Edom is known today by its Latin name, **Petra** (rock), for the city is literally carved out of the rock. Hence Jesus

gives his disciple the name Peter, saying: "You are **Peter**, and **on this rock** I will build my church." (Matthew 16:18) Another Edomite city is known by the name *Sela*, the Hebrew word for rock: "He [Amaziah] defeated ten thousand Edomites in the Valley of Salt, and he captured Sela in battle..." (II Kings 14:7)

4. Vulture or eagle?
Most modern scholars accept Israel Aharoni's identification of the Biblical bird, *nesher*, as vulture and not the eagle it was one thought to be.

"Does the vulture soar at your command, building his nest high, dwelling in the rock, lodging upon **the fastness of a jutting rock**? From there it searches for food. From afar his eyes can see. His young gulp blood; where the slain are, there is he."

(Job 39:27-30)

But it is not only the foreign nations whom God will pluck from their rocky fastnesses. The Israelites also will be unable to save themselves by hiding "in caves and holes and among the rocks, in pits and cisterns." (I Samuel 13:6):

The rocky fastness of Petra

"Lo, I am sending for many fishermen — declares
the Lord — and they shall haul them out; and after
that I will send for many hunters, and they shall
hunt them out of every mountain and out of every
hill and out of the crevices in the rocks. For My
eyes are on all their ways, they are not hidden from
My sight, nor is their wrongdoing concealed from
Me." (Jeremiah 16:16-17)

Not only the vulture utilizes the safety of a rock crevice.
David, too, used such natural fortifications in his flight from
Saul, both "in the strongholds of the groves, at the hill of

Hakhakhila south of the *yeshimon*" (I Samuel 23:19) and also "in the fastnesses of Ein Gedi" (I Samuel 23:29). No wonder that "after the Lord had saved him from the hands of all his enemies and from the hands of Saul," (II Samuel 22:1) David begins "the words of this song" with:

> "The Lord is my crag, my fastness, my deliverer! My God, my rock where I find safety; my shield, my mighty horn of rescue, my fortress and refuge!"
>
> (II Samuel 22:2-3 and Psalm 18:3)

Rock of Ages

Of all the attributes by which God has been called, *tzur* צור — rock — is one of the most commonly used in Jewish tradition. In the continuation of this psalm, David says, "The Lord lives! Blessed is **my rock**! Exalted be God, **the rock of my deliverance**." (Psalm 18:47) This epithet is also found in a number of David's psalms:

> "Be **a rock, a stronghold for me**...for You are **my rock and my fortress**." (Psalm 31:3-4)

> "Be **a sheltering rock** for me...for **You are my rock and my fortress**." (Psalm 71:3)

> "May the words of my mouth and the prayer of my heart be acceptable to You, O Lord, **my rock and my redeemer**." (Psalm 19:15)

> "O **Lord**, I call to You; **my rock**, do not disregard me." (Psalm 28:1)

> "From the end of the earth I call to You; when my heart is faint, You led me to **a rock that is high above me**. For You have been my refuge, **a tower of strength against the enemy**." (Psalm 61:3-4)

> "Truly He is **my rock and deliverance, my haven**; I shall never be shaken." (Psalm 62:3)

> "Blessed is the **Lord, my rock**, and my refuge, **my protection in whom I take shelter**." (Psalm 144:1-2)

The wild goats of Ein Gedi

5. David's desert beverages

Sometimes the water found in desert wadis is unfit to drink. Shallow, still water is a conducive medium for the rapid growth of tiny organisms that render the water unpotable to humans. A useful method of improving the taste of such water (and also of disinfecting it) is to boil fragrant plants in it that are not bitter. A common desert plant that can be brewed into a pleasant "tea" even when using foul-tasting water is the fragrant desert aster, *Asteriscus graveolens* *(bottom right)*. Surely David and his men enjoyed this "aster tea" while sitting around a campfire in the cold desert nights. But what did David do when there was no water in the wadis? He must have known that even the lightest rainfall — or a heavy dew — is sufficient to partially fill the "cups" formed by the leaves of the white squill (*Urginea maritima*) *(bottom left)* with a small amount of water that can be sipped through any handy hollow stem.

And "when Saul returned from pursuing the Philistines" and received the information that "David was in the desert of Ein Gedi," [5] he "went in search of David and his men in the direction of the rocks of the wild goats" (I Samuel 24:1-2) because he knew that these rocks were shielding David.[6]

The epithet "rock" for God is found in the Bible in various combinations in numerous instances. But it is significant that the conjunction **Rock of Israel** was first used in the Bible by David (II Samuel 23:3). The association of God with a rock was evidently born in the landscapes of the desert where the Children of Israel wandered before their entrance into the Land of Israel, as attested by the book of Deuteronomy (32:4). But it seems that the epithet filtered into Jewish liturgy of later generations from those verses in Psalms that contain David's tribute to the days when he was sheltered by the rocks in the desert.

6. The partridge and the flea

Pursued by Saul in the desert, David had two opportunities to kill him; both times David refrained from harming Saul, but chose to reason with him and attempt to prove that he had no treacherous intent. In both instances David called on the flea for help: the first time with the "cooperation" of a dead dog and the second with that of the mountain partridge.

Following the incident in which David cut off a piece of Saul's cloak in the cave, David cries out to Saul: "Against whom has the king of Israel come out? Whom are you pursuing? A dead dog? A single flea?" (I Samuel 24:14) With these words David tries to convince his pursuer that the pursued is not worth the effort, that he is worthless and poses no threat.

The second time follows the incident of the spear and the water skin which David and Avishai stole from Saul while he and his entire camp were fast asleep. Once again David tries to prove to Saul that he had him in his power but did not harm him: "Why does my lord continue to pursue his servant? What have I done, and what wrong am I guilty of?...For the king of Israel has come out to seek a single flea — as if he were hunting a partridge in the hills!" (I Samuel 26:18,20)

It seems to me that in this instance David is referring to much more than his own insignificance. The mountain partridge is a desert bird, a small relation of the common partridge found all over Israel. It is a bird familiar to all hikers in the Judean Desert, especially in the area of Ein Gedi. Its coloring blends with the ground and the stones, so it is extremely difficult to spot unless it moves and sounds its unusual calls. When it feels danger approaching, it immediately takes flight very close to ground level and disappears among the rocks or behind a hummock.

Each time I tried to focus my camera on one of these mountain partridges it managed to disappear into the background without a trace. No doubt David was familiar with this characteristic of the mountain partridge, which makes it so difficult for the hunter to enjoy its tasty flesh. The flea is notorious for its huge leaps, jumping freely between animal and human, annoying both and exceedingly difficult to catch. David must have tried, probably without much success, to kill the fleas that annoyed him in the caves where he hid. It is also reasonable to assume that he and his men tried to catch the mountain partridge for food but that it usually managed to evade them. The picture David paints for Saul contains a double message: while emphasizing what a lightweight he is in comparison to the king of Israel, David increases Saul's frustration by comparing his futile pursuit to trying to catch the flea or the mountain partridge, both of which are champions at quick evasive action and skipping from one hiding place to another.

148

The shepherd's staff

"Shepherd Your people with Your staff, Your very own flock." (Micah 7:14)

The shepherd's staff is an all-purpose tool: it is used to guide the flock, as a walking aid, and as a defensive weapon against wild animals and enemies. Various names reflect its many uses: rod, staff, crook, stave, even club and scepter. In the Hebrew Scriptures there are numerous names for this implement, suggesting perhaps that each word refers to different kinds of "sticks." But because the words are so frequently interchangeable in the original Hebrew, it is evident that they all refer to the same basic object, although it can be made in various styles and from different kinds of wood. Numerous English words are used interchangeably in the various translations of the Bible, with no consistent use of the same English word for every instance of a given Hebrew word.

In the phrase "Thy rod and Thy staff they comfort me" (Psalm 23:4) we feel the security this implement imparts, especially in "the valley of the shadow of death." Just as a cane warns a blind person of obstacles and detours in his path, so the staff enables the experienced walker to test the depth of water or mud (as attested by Jacob: "with my staff I crossed the Jordan." Genesis 32:11). The traveler who must make his way in the dark of night between the canyon walls of the "valley of the shadow of death" uses a staff to feel his way among the boulders strewn in the dry wadi. The staff acts as a brake in descending steep hills, which in the desert frequently become avalanches of stones. As a club, the staff is most effective as a defensive weapon against various attackers, whether they walk on two or four legs or crawl on their bellies. It was therefore appropriate that on the eve of the exodus from Egypt and the start of the lengthy wandering in the desert, the Israelites were commanded to eat their last meal "...[with] your sandals on your feet, and your staff (*makel* מקל) in your hand." (Exodus 12:11)

The various names and uses of the staff are found in many

places in the Bible and the sayings of the Sages. The following are just a few illustrations:

As David set out to battle Goliath:

> "He took his staff (*makel*), picked five smooth stones from the wadi and put them in his shepherd's bag...and went toward the Philistine." (I Samuel 17:40)

Benaiah son of Jehoiada, one of David's warriors, goes armed with his staff:

> "He went down against [the Egyptian] with a club (*shevet* שבט), wrenched the spear out of the Egyptian's hand, and killed him with his own spear." (II Samuel 23:21)

In the words of the prophet Micah, the staff is used to guide the flock:

> "Shepherd your people with Your staff (*shevet*), Your very own flock." (Micah 7:14)

And the prophet Zechariah uses the shepherd's staff in two ways:

> "I got two staffs (*maklot* מקלות), one of which I named Pleasant and the other Destroyer, and I proceeded to tend the sheep." (Zechariah 11:7)

The staff used to guide the flock also appears in the following midrash:

"Rabbi Eliezer said: Even though they were told by the Lord, the Children of Israel did not leave Egypt until Moses led them forth with a staff (*makel*)." (Shmot Rabbah 24, 2)

The rod and staff appear also in Isaiah:

> "Assyria, rod (*shevet*) of My anger, the staff (*matteh* מטה) of My wrath is in their hand." (Isaiah 10:5)

> "Assyria, who beats you with a rod (*shevet*) and wields his staff (*matteh*) over you..." (Isaiah 10:24)

Whoever has the staff, rod, or club in his hand can also

control the flock or the nation, and this is how the prophets express this idea:

"Rejoice not, you Philistines, because the rod (*shevet*) that chastised you is broken." (Isaiah 14:29)

"Alas, the commander's staff (*matteh*) is broken, the lordly staff (*makel*)!" (Jeremiah 48:17)

"She had stout branches (*mattot* מטות, pl.of *matteh*) fit for a ruler's scepter (*shevet*)." (Ezekiel 19:11)

The ruler's scepter (*shevet hamoshlim* שבט המושלים) appears in Jacob's blessing over Judah:

"The scepter (*shevet*) shall not depart from Judah, nor the ruler's staff (*mekhokek* מחקק) from his descendants." (Genesis 49:10)

The staff as the symbol of authority is also found in the golden scepter (*sharvit* שרביט) that King Ahasuerus extended to Esther (Esther 5:2). The Sages frequently use the word *sharvit* in the sense of an offshoot growing from the trunk or branch of a tree. But in their usage, too, there is a connection between the *sharvit*, the *matteh*, and leadership or government: "Why is the Lord, Blessed be He, called the King of glory? Because He honors those who stand in awe before Him. How?...A flesh and blood king does not give his scepter (*sharvit*) to anyone else, but the Lord, Blessed be He, gave His scepter (*sharvit*) to Moses, as it is written: And Moses took the rod (*matteh*) of God with him. (Exodus 4:20)" (Shmot Rabbah 8,1). Of special interest is the image taken from the grapevine, which sends forth long tendrils that twine around other trees: "What is this grapevine from which one *sharvit* is produced which rules over all the trees, so is Israel: one righteous man from the people of Israel shall rule from one end of the earth to the other, as is written: Now Joseph was the ruler of the land [of Egypt]. (Genesis 42:6)" (Vayikra Rabbah 36, 2)

The appellation *shevet* (שבט) or *matteh* (מטה) for each of the Twelve Tribes of Israel is usually explained as an allusion to the offshoot from a tree trunk, comparable to one meaning of the word "stock." But based on the examples given above, I believe it is more logical to see the source of these terms in the life of the shepherd who used the rod (*shevet*) or staff (*matteh*) to lead the flock. It is in the desert that these implements became the symbol of authority.

In another midrash we see the word *hoter* (חוטר) — an offshoot growing from the trunk of a tree — as a symbol of leadership, similar to the *matteh:* "Your staff (*matteh*) is the Messiah King, as it is said: And there shall come an offshoot (*hoter*) from the [trunk] of the house of Jesse. (Isaiah 11:1)" (Breshit Rabbah 85, 9)

It is interesting to compare the image used by Isaiah with that used by Jeremiah: Isaiah sees the future messiah of the house of David (Jesse's son) symbolized by the shepherd's staff which has a knob at its end, the *hoter*, usually made from an offshoot of an olive tree. Olive groves are common in the area between Bethlehem and Jerusalem. David was born in Bethlehem; Isaiah was a Jerusalemite. Isaiah's metaphor literally grows out of the ancient olive trees in this area. On the other hand, the area of Anatot, where Jeremiah was born and lived, presents a very different scene: there, in an area with far less rain, almond trees fare better than olives. Therefore when God asks Jeremiah "What do you see?" (Jeremiah 1:11), he immediately visualizes "a rod (*makel*) of an almond tree (*shaked* שקד)."

A fitting conclusion to this chapter can be found in the following midrash: "David minted a coin. And what was on that coin? A staff (*makel*) and shepherd's pouch on one side [of the coin] and a tower on the other side [of the coin]..." (Breshit Rabbah 39,11). Coins were minted of precious metals and were used far beyond the kingdom's borders. The compilers of the midrash emphasized, therefore, that even when David reached the exalted position of king, fortified Jerusalem, and built watchtowers, he saw fit to proclaim even in foreign lands that his experience in leadership was gained when he shepherded his flocks in the desert, carrying his staff, with his pouch slung on his back.

152 *Ancient olive trees near Bethlehem*

Summary

"Thou preparest a table before me... Thou anointest my head with oil, my cup runneth over." (Psalm 23:5)

153

By way of summary we return to the twenty-third psalm, which has accompanied each chapter of this book. It bears rereading:

A Psalm of David.

"The Lord is my shepherd; I shall not want.
He maketh me to lie down in green pastures;
He leadeth me beside the still waters.
He restoreth my soul;
He leadeth me in the paths of righteousness for
His name's sake.

Yea, though I walk through the valley of the
shadow of death,
I will fear no evil, for Thou art with me.
Thy rod and Thy staff they comfort me.

Thou preparest a table before me in the presence of
mine enemies;
Thou anointest my head with oil;
My cup runneth over.
Surely goodness and mercy shall follow me
all the days of my life,
And I will dwell in the house of the Lord forever."

As was noted at the beginning of this book, psalm 23 can be read on two levels: one reflects the history of David; the second hints at the different stages of Israel's history and the vision of the future as seen by the prophets of Israel.

As concerns David:

There are 72 psalms bearing the name of David. I have tried to show that many of them reflect the landscapes of the Judean Desert and the special experiences David may have had there. The twenty-third psalm, whose verses formed the headings of each chapter in this book, synthesizes in a few verses a number of these experiences. At first David was the shepherd who grazed his father's flocks in green pastures of the desert, leading his flocks to still, restful waters. Later, he was pursued by Saul in that same desert, and the psalm hints at the difficulties of orientation on the paths that encircle the multitude of confusing mountains and David's escape from Saul in the shadowed and twisted valleys. His trust in God, Who guided and protected him, finally brought him to the throne, symbolized by his anointment with oil, by the table set before him covered with plentiful food as compared to the days of meager rations in the desert, and by the cup that overflows with the juice of the grape after the days of thirst in the desert.

As concerns Israel:

The book of Psalms also contains entire poems that describe — sometimes in symbolic language — the history of the Children of Israel, emphasizing the fluctuations in their relationship to God: in the days of their slavery in Egypt, during the wandering in the desert, and as a settled farming nation in the Land of Israel.

In the process of adjustment to an agrarian life-style, idol worship spread among the people in their search for surety that their crops — especially grain, wine, and oil — would prosper in the special climatic conditions of the Land of Israel. The prophets battled against this temptation to worship other gods, which was also reflected in the growth of social and moral corruption. When they failed to change the nation's direction, the prophets saw the solution in the destruction of the existing agricultural base, together with all the concomitant urban layers, and the nation's return to a nomadic shepherding life in the desert. There everything could begin again. In the twenty-third psalm it is possible to see hints of the essence of this vision: a return to the youthful days in the desert will once again bring the nation to recognize the true Shepherd, in whose power it is to direct His flock and lead it to overcome all obstacles. Cleansed of its sins, the nation of Israel will return to the Promised Land and to farming that Land. But this time the tillers of the soil too will recognize and accept that the God of Israel is the one who gives the grain on the set table (a hint at the shewbread that was placed on the table in the Holy Temple), He is the one who anoints with olive oil, and He is the one who fills the cup with wine "to overflowing." This new life, based on a refined faith, will also bring goodness and mercy instead of the corruption and disaster that typified the era of the prophets. Then, too, will the Holy Temple in Jerusalem be recognized as the single nucleus of all the factions of the nation, to last, this time, for eternity.

INDEX ( ) Marginal entries

GENERAL INDEX